JESUS

SPEAKING

JESUS

SPEAKING

On Falling in Love with Life

GINA LAKE

Endless Satsang Foundation
www.RadicalHappiness.com

ISBN: 978-1546526780

Cover photo: © Subbotina/CanStockPhoto.com
Copyright © 2017 by Gina Lake

Contents

PREFACE

This book, given to me by Jesus, is intended to serve a slightly different purpose than the other books I've been given from Jesus. Unlike those other books, this one was created by speaking into a recorder and then transcribing those words. Consequently, it reads a little differently than the books that were intended as written works. The audio version of this book, of me channeling these words, is also available. The print book has been edited for clarity, but the tone of the audiobook has been retained.

My hope is that the audiobook and this companion book will give you the experience of having a relationship with the wise and gentle being we've known as Jesus the Christ, as he speaks to you as if you were sitting in his presence. The experience of an unconditionally loving relationship with a wise being is what I experience when I channel, and I hope it's your experience as well, as you read or listen to these words.

Words, whether they are spoken or written, can transmit consciousness as well as speak to the unconscious mind in a way that can heal and reprogram it. May you experience the peace and love these words are pointing to and may they help you fall in love with life. And now, it's time for Jesus to speak.

Gina Lake
January, 2017

INTRODUCTION

I am the one you have known as Jesus the Christ. I am speaking to you now through this channel to help you to know of my presence and to feel my presence in your life more fully. I want you to know that I exist here, in another dimension, that I am eternally present and continue to be the servant for all that is good, and that you — like me — are also eternal and will continue to exist once you leave this temporary body.

You are so much more than you realize. I was but an example of what you are capable of as a human being. But in essence, you, like me, are much more than a human being. You are an eternal being. My intention in speaking to you in this way is to help you realize your true nature and to live as the best human being you can be. The challenges are great in the human body, but you can overcome them and become the loving and strong being you are meant to be.

By making a practice of doing just a few things, you can become more aligned with your own divinity, with the goodness within you. In this book, I have laid out some of those things. These simple practices and understandings will help you be happy, more loving, and more at peace.

Happiness, love, and peace are the signs that you have arrived Home. You are meant to be happy, loving, and at peace. Allow me to be your guide Home. It is my deepest honor to serve you in this way, for in doing so, I am serving the Whole and giving glory to the Father, who has created all of life. And now, I will present a very important understanding, that of Grace...

CHAPTER 1
Grace

The Hand of Grace

Grace is the hand of God in life. Yes, there is a hand of God in life. The first hurdle in recognizing Grace is recognizing that there is a hand of God in life. There is Grace. There is so much Grace in life that it permeates everything. There isn't a creation that isn't moved by Grace. There isn't an event that doesn't have Grace behind it. Even events that you might call ego-driven, Grace is allowing those events to happen. So there is Grace causing things to happen, and there is Grace allowing things to happen according to one's free will. This will is essentially the will of the ego, the false self, for there is no other will besides Thy will except the ego's will. Everything else is Thy will. Everything else is Grace.

So you could say that Grace is Thy will, but Grace is more than will or intention; it is the actual movement of God in life. I say the "hand" of God because hands move, don't they? Hands affect life. Hands manipulate life. They push, they pull, they shape, and they create. So it is with the hand of God, with Grace: It shapes, it manipulates, and of course it does allow. So it is either acting in life or standing back and allowing the false self, driven by the ego, to act and have its experience and make its choices and experience the results of those choices.

Always there is this dance going on between Thy will, or Grace, and the ego's, or false self's, will and what it chooses to do, what it chooses to create, and how it chooses to use its energy and will. So this makes life interesting. There is both a false self that is moved through life based on programming, including the ego, which itself is programming, and then there is life itself moving its creations in life. This makes life more interesting, doesn't it?

The hand of God is moving in life, and it is much more interesting for the hand of God to move in a world where there is free will, free choice, where there is push-back, you could say, where there is something else choosing. And yet, ultimately it is the hand of God that shapes life. Ultimately, the hand of God has its way with life.

The only thing that you, as a false self or ego, is able to accomplish is what this hand of God allows you to accomplish. If it were not for that, you could accomplish nothing. In fact, many of the times you fail to accomplish what you would like to, it is simply because you are not being allowed to accomplish it, not because you aren't working hard enough or not thinking the right thoughts or willing it adequately. You are simply not allowed to have what you want all the time.

What is this that doesn't allow you to have what you want? It is Grace. You hardly think that Grace would be something that gets in your way. You think of Grace as a positive force, as a helping hand. But sometimes Grace stops you. It halts you. It holds its hand up and says: "No. Stop. You can't go this way. You can't have this." So even that is Grace. Even that is the most beautiful, loving hand of God doing the wisest and most loving thing it can do for you.

So whatever happens in life is the hand of Grace. It is either the hand of Grace helping you along, providing you with opportunities, ideas, inspiration, and other people who help you, or it's the hand that stops you from going in a direction that would not be supportive of your overall growth or of benefit to the Whole—because Grace, this hand of God, is functioning for the Whole, of which you are a part.

You are a cog in the wheel in the cosmos, and the cogs must work a certain way for the universe to function properly. This hand of God is the grease that greases the wheels, and it also makes sure the wheels stay on their tracks so that they do their proper job, play their proper role, and hold their proper place in the universe.

So, you see, you are very important. Just as a cog in the machine can take the entire machine down, your missteps or going off the plan can keep the Whole from functioning as it's meant to and evolving in the direction it's meant to. So sometimes it is necessary for Grace to stop people from going in a certain direction or from making certain choices, or to prevent the fruits of those choices from working out. This is a very big job that Grace has—a very big job indeed! It is an unimaginable intelligence that is operating behind the scenes here, this hand of God, the God whose hand this is—it is an unimaginable intelligence.

And it is a benevolent one. Grace is benevolent. Even when it appears to not be benevolent, it is most benevolent. It is absolutely benevolent. It is unceasingly benevolent. It can be nothing but benevolent. This is very good news! The universe, the creation, the cosmos, all of creation, of which you are an eternal part, is benevolent—absolutely and completely benevolent. Anything that appears otherwise is nothing that is actually shaping life, that is having any real power in life. It is only being allowed to act for the time being.

Any so-called evil that exists is being allowed by Grace because it is part of the evolution for those involved in this evil. They are evolving as they need to in order to be the appropriate cog in this wheel of the cosmos. There is a learning, an adjusting, and an experimentation that goes on with people before they fall in line and discover their purpose and discover Grace and discover that they wish to align with Grace. Before that, their free will takes them in all sorts of directions, and this is allowed, for the time being — not forever.

Built into creation is a natural learning to align with Grace, with love, with the benevolence behind all life. Everyone eventually learns this, and that, too, is Grace. Built into creation is a learning to function from love. You all eventually learn to function from love. This is great Grace. Grace teaches you to love, and it sometimes teaches through pain: pain you created through choices that caused pain, suffering you created by believing mistaken beliefs and by going in directions that were hurtful to yourself or others.

Grace allows you to make these mistakes so that you never make them again. That's a beautiful thing, isn't it? You only have to make these mistakes a few times, and then you're done with them forevermore.

Your eternal self will always remember to go with love. This will never be forgotten once it is learned.

So you are all very, very blessed by this hand of God, very blessed by Grace. Grace is taking care of each and every one of you perfectly. It is perfectly standing by you and giving you everything you need to evolve to the next step, and then the next, and the next. Grace never leaves your side. It never gets weary. It is always patient, always loving, always compassionate. In this way, it teaches you to be loving, to be patient, to be compassionate.

Once you discover that Grace is behind life, everything changes. You can evolve much more quickly, much more happily, and much more safely too, because the only lack of safety you perceive in life is caused by your own egoic perceptions, your belief that life is not taking care of you or won't take care of you properly. That is a lie. It is a misperception, a misunderstanding, an inability to see the hand of God in your life. Once you recognize that hand, you realize that you have always been safe, you have always been taken care of, and that life has time and time again picked you up off the ground and dusted you off and sent you on your way.

You may not have liked falling down. You may not even like the direction you are sent, but that is a misperception to see it that way, to see falling down as a problem or as something that shouldn't have happened, or to see change or going in a new direction as something undesirable. That is your own internal, attitudinal problem. It's not a real problem.

Life is always wise in how it delivers its lessons and picks you up and gives you a new life in place of the old one. Life is unbelievably wise and compassionate. It knows exactly what you need, and it gives you exactly what you need. It might give you a lesson, which you might not like. It might give you a challenge, which you also might not like. It might give you a gift, which you will undoubtedly like, or maybe you won't like that either. But your liking or not liking what life is delivering is, in a sense, your problem, your self-creation. If your attitude were different, you would not experience a difficulty, a change, a challenge, and certainly not a gift as a problem.

The egoic self experiences much of life as undesirable and a problem. Every step, every turn it takes, it has difficulty with. The ego argues with life. It doesn't like it. It chooses to perceive life as it is unfolding as problematic, as undesirable, as something it doesn't like or want. Well, that is the ego's problem. The ego generates the problem of not liking life.

Life is not unlikeable. In its essence, life is perfect and lovable and wise. And you're here to discover that. You're here to discover the perfection of the life you are living and the life that everyone is given. It's hard for your ego to see the perfection, but you have to learn to see this. That is the work here on this plane of existence. That is the learning here—to see the perfection, to see that life is good, to see that Grace is infusing everything.

There isn't a moment, a second, that isn't infused with Grace, care, protection, and love from this benevolent Intelligence that is guiding all of it. Grace is everywhere. Grace is eternal. Grace has been everywhere, will be everywhere, and cannot be anything but infusing every single moment of life, because the very nature of life is goodness. So everything this life force does in relation to its creation—in relation to itself—is ultimately good, whether it can be recognized as that or not.

The only thing that doesn't recognize life as good would be the programming, the ego, the misperceptions of the false self. Once these misperceptions are seen through, then you begin to love life, you begin to accept it, you begin to grow with it, align with it, flow with it. Then you can be in the flow and love life and enjoy it just the way it is, with nothing needing to be changed, nothing out of place, nothing wrong—everything just so, just as it is, just as it is meant to be.

This doesn't mean that life is predetermined when I say that life is perfect just as it is, because there are many ways that this perfection can unfold, and the Intelligence behind life doesn't necessarily know exactly how life will unfold in this plane of existence, or in other planes for that matter.

Life is free-flowing and there are multiple possibilities — infinite possibilities — for how anything can play out based on what individuals might choose and the choices that are allowed and the choices that are stopped. The shaping of this hand of Grace in coordination with free will creates many, many possibilities that are always changing and unpredictable. Hence, there are many, many multiverses, many possible alternative universes, in which every possible choice and every possible imagination is actually being lived out. This is great enjoyment for the Intelligence.

Behind each and every possible universe, each and every possible dimension, there is love and there is benevolence. There is no such thing as a universe that does not have benevolence behind it. It may appear that a universe does not because it is so drenched in egoic negativity, but that is only temporary, because even those universes are evolving toward greater goodness, greater peace, and greater love. There is no such thing as a Hell. There are temporary places that are hellish. The individuals in those places are learning love, just as you are. It's not different there. It's only worse.

So dear ones, you are being taken care of, you are always loved, and you are always guided. Your lives are perfectly shaped by a higher intelligence that knows exactly what you need to evolve to the next stage. You get to choose, to some extent, how you do that and what you experience. But ultimately, the deeper plan, the blueprint, is not in your hands but in the hands of God.

You are the beloved sons and daughters of this great Intelligence. You *are* this great Intelligence made manifest as men and women, as children, and as every single creature. But you are very special because you do have free will. You are sentient in a way that other creations are not, and there is a certain responsibility that goes with that. So choose wisely, dear ones, and know that you are being encouraged in every moment to choose wisely and that you are being given answers that will cause you greater fulfillment if you only listen. So, please, do try to tune in and listen to this great hand of Grace that is operating in every moment of your life.

Grace in Life

Grace operates in everyone's life in many different ways. The most common way, perhaps, is through other people. Other people help you, give you advice, inspire you, and model what you can be or what you can do. You learn from others, you grow from others; they are your teachers, and they are your helpers — and you are theirs.

This is how the Whole evolves. This is how the Whole supports itself. You are all part of the Whole, and the parts assist the other parts. You are all instruments of Grace, instruments of the Divine, eyes of God, mouths of God. Everything you do or say has the potential to be infused with God, with Grace. It has the potential to be Grace working through you.

Another possibility also exists, of course, and that is that you act on your own free will according to the thoughts that run through your head. These are the ego's thoughts, the conditioned self's thoughts. These thoughts attempt to guide your life. They attempt to tell you how to live your life, how to move, how to act, what to say, when to say it, and what to do. The thoughts that run through your head try to tell you how to live your life.

These thoughts are not the hand of God, although nothing can be outside of God, of course. Rather, this is an alternate will, a will that sets itself against Thy will in many cases, but not always. Your personal will is often in opposition to Thy will. When it is, you suffer, because you, as part of the Whole and an instrument of the Whole, cannot possibly be happy—you're not built to be happy—when you oppose the Whole, the evolution of the Whole, and your role in it.

We could call Thy will the flow. When you oppose the flow (your individual flow, which meshes with the flow of others in the Whole and creates the entire flow), you suffer. You may still end up having to follow that flow, because the flow will usually have its way with people, one way or the other. But it is often not pleasant if you oppose the flow.

If you are aligned with the flow, it's pleasant, it's enjoyable. You feel fulfilled, and there's joy in being in the flow. You're at ease, you're at peace, and love flows easily from you. When you are not in the flow, however, you're struggling. It's like fighting the current of a river. It's hard work. You suffer, you strain, you struggle. But Grace allows this. There's room for this struggle, and yet ultimately Grace will have its way with you. Grace will have you go its way. One way or the other, it will bring you around.

Some of the deepest challenges and difficulties in life are the hand of Grace bringing people around, showing them the direction they need to go in instead of the direction they *are* going in. The hand of Grace is always kind, in that the direction that it wants you to go in is good for you. But getting you to change your direction isn't always easy. It can cause more struggle on your part and more pain until you accept that direction.

You don't really know what's ahead, so it's natural to struggle against it. You don't trust what's ahead. You don't trust the hand of Grace. And yet, if you did, life would be so much easier. You would relax and know that where Grace is taking you is good and right for you and for everyone involved.

What's right for you, from the standpoint of Grace, can't be anything but right for everyone else involved. This is often hard to see when others are not happy with you making a certain choice or taking a certain direction that you feel is aligned with your higher purpose, and they don't agree with that. It can be hard to see that this choice to follow your Heart is also a positive choice for them. It's also the right choice for them. It may not feel like the right choice *to* them, but that doesn't mean it isn't.

Just know that you cannot make a choice that is in alignment with your own Heart, with the Whole, without it also being aligned with everyone else's life purpose, everyone else's growth, no matter how difficult it might seem. Difficulty is not the measure by which you should judge an experience. If an experience is difficult, that doesn't mean it shouldn't be happening. It *should*. And your task is to make that experience less difficult by changing your attitude within that situation or by making choices that will ease the difficulty within that situation.

A difficulty is like being stuck in an eddy in the river of life. You go around and around and struggle and get nowhere until you surrender something: a point of view, a mistaken idea, a desire that's not worthy of you, or something else that's in the way of you being in the flow.

There is no difficulty but what you create in your own sense of the situation. There are challenges, but challenges are meant to be. There are challenges of your own making, and there are challenges of God's making. Either way, there is something to be learned. When it's learned, the difficulty releases. Either the situation is no longer experienced as a difficulty, or things change, and the situation is no longer difficult. One thing or the other changes, either your attitude shifts or the situation itself shifts.

Very often, it's that your own attitude shifts the situation, as you come to see things differently and come to make some different choices. So difficulties are like a puzzle for you to discover the truth. Once the truth is discovered, you either accept the difficulty or the situation itself changes.

Difficulties are Grace, and the answers or solutions to those difficulties are Grace as well. You are here to experience the Grace of all of it: the Grace of the difficulty, the Grace of finding the solution, and the Grace of being released from the difficulty. This is life, isn't it? This is growth. What would life be without such experiences of challenge and difficulty? It would be a lazy ride down the river. Apparently life, at least life in this third dimension for the time being, is meant to be more than a lazy ride down the river with no paddling required.

You are required to paddle. You are required to choose, and you are required to learn from those choices. You cannot help but learn from those choices. It would be impossible to *not* learn something from your choices. That is Grace as well. It's Grace that you learn from your choices. It's Grace that you have a choice. It's Grace that there are dilemmas in which you are forced to choose.

Another way that Grace shows up in your life — a very prominent way, a very close to home way — is in your inner inspiration, your insights, your intuition, a sense of purpose, a sense of strength, and courage. All of the finest qualities you have as a human being are Grace. They get you by — if you use them. And you are here to learn to use them. Learning to tap into these qualities is what the challenges are all about. The difficulties challenge you to find your strength, your courage, your patience, your love, your responsibility, and your compassion in the midst of it all.

The Grace is that you have these things. The Grace is that you are powerful and loving beings. You can accomplish more than you realize. You are stronger than you realize, you are more courageous than you realize, and you are wiser than you realize! There is no shortage of any of these things within you. You are given all the tools you need to navigate this life.

You are never left short, and this is something you have to learn along the way—that you have these things. They are not that hidden from you, only a little. You can find them if you look, if you trust, if you notice. Other people around you are the models for these qualities. Other people show you strength, courage, wisdom, and patience, and in so doing, teach you these things.

Life is a setup for you to win, and that is Grace. It is not a setup for you to lose, as it sometimes seems. Sometimes you do lose, but that is always only temporary. Then the challenge is to see that it's temporary and to know that winning is always possible, that something good can always come from whatever you experience. This is faith, isn't it: faith in the goodness of life, faith in Grace, faith that you will be carried through by the qualities within you that you have been given—the courage and the strength, the patience and the compassion, and the wisdom.

Your inner wisdom is the hand of Grace guiding you in this life. You are never alone. There is always a guiding hand. It is a guiding voice, except that it doesn't come into your mind like the voice in your head. It's a more subtle voice. It isn't a voice that has words but a voice of knowing, a voice of clear seeing. Sometimes you just know things.

What is it that knows things? What is this mysterious thing in you that knows, that has wisdom, that moves through life? How is it you survive as well as you do? How is it you navigate this life, with so many potential dangers, and you come out so unscathed? The hand of Grace is there catching you when you fall, moving obstacles out of your way, showing you the way, leading you, pushing you, helping you, providing helpers and information, inspiration, and courage—everything you need to move forward on your path and to stay aligned with the Whole, with your life purpose within this Whole.

When you fall off track from this purpose, Grace gives you a little nudge or it blocks you or halts you altogether, and it points you in another direction. You need to learn to read the signs to see how Grace is guiding you. How does it steer you? How is it steering you? Is it stopping you? Is it freeing the way? Is it helping you in a certain direction? These are the things you need to notice to discover the way.

You have to be like good trackers and notice the signs. Which way am I supposed to go? Look and notice and observe. Where are you receiving help? Where is the way being eased? What are you motivated to do? What are you excited about doing? Where is your joy? These are all signs to go in that direction.

The hand of Grace is very much in everyone's life, shaping it. It's easy to think that you are in control and that you can shape and create your life the way you want. That is the ego's desire, wish, and imagination. But anyone who has been in life long enough can quite easily see that life has its own agenda.

Everyone's life has a certain momentum and direction, and you aren't in control of that. You aren't in control of the influences, the help, or the opportunities you receive or do not receive. Many things are not up to you, not in your control, and you have no say about them, no matter how much you would like to have a say.

The very good news is that when you don't have a say in life, when you don't seem to have the control you would like, that is good for you. The hand of Grace is taking the wheel, taking control from you. Grace has control, and it is taking you where you most want to go, whether you realize that or not. It's taking you to where your deepest happiness and fulfillment lie. You can trust that. You can take your hands off the steering wheel and let the hand of Grace steer. It knows where you are going — you don't. Your ego pretends to know. It has an opinion about it, but that opinion is not useful guidance, and it won't get you there. It won't get you to a place that will lead to happiness and fulfillment. But the hand of Grace will.

Thy will is taking everyone to a place of fulfillment and happiness, but you have to allow it to do that. Some people hold very tightly to their desires for their life to be a certain way. The hand of Grace will allow this for a while so that you can have that experience until you realize that happiness and fulfillment do not lie in that direction. Then Grace will take the wheel from you, or you will gladly surrender it.

So life will have its way with you, and that's a good thing. It leads to happiness and fulfillment, a deeper fulfillment than you can ever get from following your own desires and ideas of what your life should look like. You are in good hands.

The Voice of Grace

Grace's voice is not heard with the ears or the mind, or rarely, but with the Heart. Grace works through your intuition, through the area known as the heart center, or simply through the body. There is a download, of sorts, that happens in the body, of a knowing. Suddenly, you just know something, you sense something, you feel something, not with your emotions but on a deeper level.

Grace works in this way to guide you. It works through knowings, through nudges, through a sense of yes, through a sense of rightness, and through your intuition. Suddenly an idea pops into your mind, but your mind didn't produce it. It came from some deeper place within you, and it showed up as an idea.

Such ideas feel very different than the ideas of the ego's thought-stream, the voice in your head. Ideas that come from your ego or conditioning don't necessarily uplift you and excite you. But ideas that pop into your mind from a deeper place, from your intuition, are felt like a lightbulb going on, a sense of yes, a sense of knowing, a sudden idea, an inspiration.

These you can trust. These are trusty guides for how to live your life. If you follow such signals, you can't go wrong. They're guiding you to a path that is in alignment with your soul's purpose and with the

Whole. Anytime you listen to your intuition, you are aligning yourself with Thy will, with something greater than yourself.

People often ask, "How can I tell the difference between my intuition and my thoughts?" Thoughts in your thought-stream feel very different from the inspiration, the urges, the yeses, the lightbulbs going on. Intuitions feel very positive. The voice in your head, most of the time, doesn't feel very positive. It feels confusing or just plain negative. The voice in your head is a voice that guides you out of fear, rules, and shoulds.

There is a place for rules and shoulds, but they aren't good guides for how to live your life, for what path to follow, for what direction to go. They might be good for crossing the street. They might be good for how to do something in the most efficient way, but they aren't good guides for where to go, when to go, how to go, or what will make you happy or give you fulfillment. Only your intuition can guide you in this way and bring you a life of greater joy, happiness, love, and fulfillment.

Everyone needs to learn to live according to their intuition. They need to learn to trust it. You do this by practicing listening to your intuition. The only way you can hear your intuition is by not listening to the noisy commentary that goes on in your head in most moments. You can't listen to two things at once, so if you're busy listening to your egoic mind, the voice in your head, you won't be able to hear anything else.

Hearing the intuition is a little bit different than the usual kind of hearing because the intuition doesn't speak to you in words, and it isn't heard by your ears. So it's a different kind of listening that you need to do. It's a listening with the Heart, you could say. Just as listening is an openness, a readiness, and a willingness to receive sound, listening with your Heart is an openness, a readiness, and a willingness to receive information from a more subtle level, from the Heart.

You're listening, not for a sound, but for a knowing. You're waiting and making room and space for a knowing to arise. However, knowings don't necessarily arise just because you have opened up space for them. They arise in their own time, when they're needed, when they're necessary. But if you practice leaving space in your life to listen, you will catch these knowings much more readily than if you don't leave space. If you're so busy listening to your mind, there will be no room for your deeper self to communicate its wisdom to you. You have to make space to allow its wisdom to arise and be heard.

This wisdom arises in its own time. The more present you are, that is, the more quiet you are inside and the less involved you are with your egoic mind, the more readily you'll be able to catch this wisdom, these knowings, when they do arise. So it's very important that you be present in your life as much as possible so that when the time comes for these knowings to arise, you will be able to notice them.

Furthermore, it will be much easier for you to follow that wisdom and guidance if you're not busy with your egoic mind. If you're not following your mind, you'll be more likely to be available to follow this deeper guidance. But if you are in the habit of following your mind and letting it guide your life, then you will question this wisdom and guidance and wonder if it is trustworthy and if you are hearing correctly—because if you listen to the mind too much, it will talk you out of your inner guidance.

Many people do hear their intuition and are aware of what it is saying to them, but they don't trust it enough to follow it. And the mind is always ready with confusing advice and reasons why trusting your intuition won't work or won't be good or won't be useful. Its job is to talk you out of following the truth, following your intuition.

The egoic mind has another plan, another agenda, and that is to get you to achieve its goals for comfort, security, status, material things, power, and control. Those are the things the ego is most interested in. It's not interested in peace, love, or happiness. It's interested in happiness in the sense that it believes that power, comfort, security, and so on will bring happiness. But those things don't bring a lasting happiness.

For the lasting happiness that everyone is seeking, you have to align with the goals that come from the deeper self: the goals for peace, love, and fulfillment through aligning with one's soul's purpose. It will be difficult to follow your life's purpose, to align with the Whole, if you are completely involved with this voice in your head, because it is seeking more superficial achievements.

So if you want true happiness, you'll have to look beyond the egoic mind and listen more deeply to a subtler voice, the voice of your intuition. Although this voice is subtle, when you give it your attention, it becomes less subtle and more clear. So the less involved you are with your egoic mind, the easier it is to pick up on this intuition and to know which direction it is pointing you in.

If you don't catch these subtle intuitions right away, your intuition will continue to deliver the messages until you do. So it's not that you only receive this guidance once, and if you miss it, you're out of luck. You receive this guidance on an ongoing basis as often and as much as you need until you heed it. Grace is very patient. It patiently delivers the same message until you receive it. It patiently guides you to wherever you need to go next.

The information you receive from Grace is on a moment-to-moment basis. It provides information that you need only for the upcoming future and upcoming direction. You are not given the entire picture of what your life is going to look like in the future. The mind, on the other hand, paints a picture for you, and says, "This is how it should look" or "This is how I want it to look," and it gives you a fantasy of the future. It pretends that this future is real and attainable.

Intuition doesn't work like this. It works on a need-to-know basis, a moment-to-moment basis. It brings you the knowing that you need in the moment. It does give you some inklings of the future from time to time, as you need, but you never know the specifics of how your life is going to look going forward.

This is a little like driving blind. You don't really know where you are going, but you don't need to know, because the hand of Grace is steering. It is taking you where you need to go, and it knows exactly how to do this in the most graceful and elegant way. So you don't need to know anything more than what you are already given intuitively. That's such a relief, really, because that's less complicated than what the mind presents to you. The mind gives you the impression that you need to plan and figure everything out ahead of time—but you don't. You don't need to know. You don't need to figure it out.

There's a place for planning, of course, but you can't plan your future. You can't plan a future that doesn't exist. You can plan for a meeting you're having next Tuesday, but you can't plan your future a year from now or five years from now or even one month from now. You don't really know where you will be then, where things will be then. So planning is useful only short-term.

When your intuition develops, you begin to hear it and feel it very strongly. It becomes very compelling. You don't want to go against it, and you feel you can't go against it. You know that if you go against it, you'll only be unhappy. You *have* to follow the sense of rightness that you're experiencing.

The voice of Grace sometimes comes through other people. They open their mouths and say something that feels just right and you know is true for you. Sometimes when a person's intuition isn't getting through to them, Grace uses other people to get through to them. It plants an idea into their intuition, and they feel it and speak it.

So other people are one of the main ways that you receive messages and guidance from Grace. These messages can be trusted when they land in your body in the same way that your own intuition does. They land in a way that just feels right. You just know. Everyone knows what their intuition feels like.

Another way the voice of Grace might operate is through a book or some other media that delivers information that you need just when you needed it. Everyone has had that experience. It's quite common, really: You hear a song on the radio, and the words in that song "click" with something in your experience, and you realize something.

There are many signs like that in your life that communicate what you need to understand. They trigger a knowing inside of you. This is the voice of Grace. The voice of Grace speaks to you in all sorts of ways: through your own intuition, through other people's voices, and through signs, information, and media. And, of course, Grace might also speak through individuals such as channels, psychics, healers, therapists, and others whose job it is to be a mouthpiece for Spirit, a helper for Grace, a deliverer of Grace. You are being taken care of in so many different ways! If you are at all willing to hear the voice of Grace, you will most certainly manage to.

Making an intention that you wish to hear the voice of Grace and praying that you be aligned with this deeper knowing and that you catch this deeper knowing when it arises will help you do so. It's always important to make that intention. Making an intention is the first step in receiving whatever it is you are intending.

So if you are having trouble moving out of the egoic mind and listening deeper within yourself, ask for help with this and take part in exercises or activities that help you move out of your busy mind and into the present moment, into the stillness and quiet where you are able to hear your intuition. Practice moving out of the mind and into that quiet, still place. Make an effort, take some time, practice meditation, and that will help. Do these things, and you will, more and more, be able to align with that which you truly are and with the Grace that is leading you and carrying you along.

This is not that difficult to do once you see that the only thing in the way of hearing the voice of Grace is that you are too busy hearing the voice in your head. Find ways to turn down the volume of the voice in your head and turn away from it, and your life will go much better. It will be much easier for you to align with your true path and do what you came here to do. Doing that is the greatest happiness and the greatest peace. It is what everyone is looking for—the deeper happiness that comes from fulfilling their part in the Whole.

How Grace Is Delivered

There is a hand of Grace, and attached to this hand is an arm, you could say, which is attached to the "body and brain" of God. So there are intermediary forces that intervene to administer Grace from the mind of God. This "arm" represents forces that are active in every one of your lives, much more than you can ever imagine. These forces *are* you, in a sense, but you are not aware of them for the most part. But they *are* you. They stem from the mind of God, from the Whole.

These forces, however, have a certain intelligence of their own, a certain identity, but not an identity like you have. They don't think of themselves as separate from the Whole; and yet, they do have a function and a sense of themselves as energy beings who have a service to perform. They perform this service with great love and attention. What they are attending to is your very own soul and the unfolding of your life plan. That is their sole job. They are called guides, spirit guides, spirit helpers, other dimensional beings, or light beings. They are not really angels, who have a different sort of purpose. Angels don't usually guide individuals.

These spirit guides are the intermediaries between you and God, you and your plan. They administer and help to bring about the unfolding of your soul's plan.

They do this primarily through your intuition, but they use other means as well. They use people, signs, feelings of joy, inspiration, upliftment, ideas, and information to move you along and help you unfold as you are meant to. They manage the flow of the river of life. They don't cause the flow to go, but they help ensure that the flow moves in the direction it is meant to. And, as I said, they do this primarily by working through your intuition.

Knowing something about these beings may be of interest to you. They do not have personalities any longer, although they can take on a personality if that serves a purpose. For instance, in speaking with you through a channel, they may take on a personality so that you experience them more personally, more humanly. But they are not at all human. Your human form is a material form. They do not have a material form, they do not have a personality, they do not have a will of their own, and they do not have emotions as you do, unless you consider unconditional love to be an emotion.

Unconditional love is what they operate from. They operate out of love for you, out of love for the Whole, out of love for God. That is their purpose. As they serve you, they evolve into more perfect servants of God. So there is an evolution and, therefore, a certain hierarchy among them.

Some are less skillful, you could say, in which case, they are being shadowed or assisted by others who are more experienced until they are able to work on their own. They, too, are learning, growing, and evolving. It is possible for them to make mistakes, but it is unlikely they will make any mistakes of importance, and they can very quickly modify things to ameliorate their mistake.

So these forces can be trusted. Your mind is not trustworthy, however. Even your intellect is not that trustworthy, since the knowledge in your intellect is limited. You don't know the nature of the universe. You don't know so many things. So even your intellect is quite limited. But certainly you can't trust your egoic mind, so what is there left to trust but your intuition, your Heart?

The beings who watch over you move you through your intuition. They know exactly how to do this and when. *When* is a very important factor. *When* they deliver the intuition, inspiration, guidance, or knowing is extremely important, because there is a time for everything, and everything does come in its own time. They are the timekeepers in the sense that they are the ones who deliver exactly what you need exactly when you need it, and not before. You can trust that, and you can perhaps remember that: If you don't know what to do or you don't understand something or you can't see through to the future, then it is perhaps not time to know or to understand or to see that.

Always you are given exactly what you need — and no more. To be given more than what you need could only be confusing, more fodder for the egoic mind to confuse you or create resistance. For instance, if you were told that you would become president of the United States — if you knew that at the depths of your being — your ego could cause a lot of problems with that information. It might sabotage the entire event.

This is one reason you are not given information about the future that you think might be useful. For the most part, information about the future would be misused by your egoic mind. It would be used to confuse you, to puff you up, or cause resistance or create other misunderstandings. So you can perhaps appreciate that it's for your own good to not know many of the things that you don't know.

Very occasionally, you are given, intuitively or through a psychic or channel, some piece of information that might be helpful for you to know. This is what's determined by your guides. They must be wise enough to know what to give and what not to give you, not only when to give it to you, but also how much of the truth to give you about your future or even about a current event.

For instance, if you are in a relationship, how much about that relationship is good for you to know while you're first beginning it? Couldn't any amount of information change the outcome? What if someone is not the princess or prince charming you hope him or her to be, and yet, the relationship is a very important one and your soul wants you to stay with it, and then a psychic tells you that this is not your princess or prince charming, so don't bother? That would be an interference in your plan if your soul wanted you to pursue that relationship for some other reason.

So even psychics and channels can get in the way of the flow. They may give you information that is not in your best interest to have. When that happens, those guiding you have to work with that. They have to make adjustments in your life plan to accommodate whatever choices you make with your free will. And so it is not easy at all to be a guide. It takes thousands and thousands, really millions, of lifetimes before you are advanced enough to be a guide of a third dimensional human being. It takes a very long time to gain this wisdom.

Those guiding you continue to receive guidance from higher dimensional beings beyond them. This is how the work of the universe is carried out: Those "above" help those "below," and then they help those below them, and so on. It is a vast hierarchy, and the wisdom and love at the base of it is unimaginable. You cannot imagine the wisdom and love those beings have for you, for life, and for God as they carry out their tasks.

You can speak to these individuals. You can make an intention to connect with them, and that will make their job easier. It will be much easier for them to work with you if you consciously align yourself with them by speaking to them, inviting them to make themselves known more in your life, and opening to their intuitions. By stating and intending this, it will happen.

Your role in this is very important, because as powerful, wise, and able as they are, they cannot transgress your free will. If your free will closes them out, they are out, at least to some extent. They can never be totally put out of your life. You wouldn't be able to function. You would lose your way without them. So you can't push them aside. No matter what you do, they are unconditionally loving and serving you. But you can bring them closer by inviting them, and you can make yourself more aware of them by opening to them, stating your openness to them, and making room in your life to listen to them.

This information is being given because it is important and helpful—valuable—for you to understand that you are part of a much greater family, and this family takes care of itself. It is not at all like what the mind would have you believe—that this is a dangerous world and universe, and it is just you against it all, fighting for survival. This is not how it is. You are intimately connected to All That Is through these beings on various levels, who are working to uplift and evolve you and bring about the lessons and experiences you need.

There is benevolence in all of it, and trusting this is very important. Knowing that there are benevolent beings guiding you in every single moment is very important. Then you can begin to relax, you can begin to trust life, and you can begin to let go of the egoic mind, which tells you not to trust life and gives you fearful messages.

Those messages are really the only thing to be feared, in a sense. But you don't need to fear them either, like the saying, "The only thing to fear is fear itself." This is so very true, but I would also say not to fear, fear itself, because fear is a mirage. Fear is an imagination that becomes real when you believe it. You create that fearful reality by believing it. But you can just as easily un-create it by not believing it.

So I'm giving you something else to believe: Believe that this is a benevolent universe. Believe that the most wise and loving beings you can ever imagine—way beyond your imagination—are intimately tied to you and helping your life unfold as it needs to. Know this in the depths of your soul, and this life will be made much easier for you. Connect with this level as best you can, feel it, and trust it, because you are in very good hands.

The hands of Grace are the best of hands. They have no ill will toward you. Your mind, on the other hand, is misguided. It will give you all the wrong guidance. It will take you off the path, out of the flow, and into a very unhappy place, a fearful place. So don't go there. Stay, instead, in this very present moment, where there is nothing to fear. Even though you don't know what is going to happen next, that doesn't matter. You don't need to know. Life is trustworthy and bringing you exactly the experiences you need and all of the information, wisdom, strength, and courage you need to go about this life.

CHAPTER 2
Prayer

Prayer Connects

Prayer connects you to the unseen forces that guide you in your daily life. You are always connected to these forces, but prayer opens the door on your side to allow them to work more closely with you. Prayer is a way of saying, "I am open, willing, and ready to receive whatever I need to receive to unfold my plan, to evolve, to learn my lessons, to heal, to serve, to love, to have."

Prayer is a way of acknowledging your co-creation with the Creator. You are instruments of God's creation. You are instruments that interact with creations, and you are creators yourself, in your own right. You are a means by which the Creator creates.

To the extent that you connect with the Creator, you can create in alignment with the Creator. To the extent that you do not connect with the Creator, it is allowed for you to create what you choose on the basis of your own will. You are allowed to create in that way as well. So you could say there are two kinds of creation: creation on the part of the ego, or personal self, which is based on conditioning, and creation according to Thy will, the Creator's will. The only way you can know what the Creator's will is, is to connect in some way to the Creator, to the Oneness, to God, to whatever you would like to call this immense force that is behind all creation.

This force is not separate from you. It's the same as you. You are an extension of it in the world. There is no separation between this extension and the Creator itself, just as there is no separation between the hand and the rest of the body. So you are like that. You are like the hand of the Creator in this world, moving about and manipulating life, creating, choosing, doing, making, manufacturing. You are the instrument of God, and this instrument is not separate from God. It *is* God. It is an extension of God, not separate in any way.

There is a sense of being separate because you've forgotten your origin. You don't realize you are connected to All That Is. That is as it is meant to be, for the time being. Then you are meant to rediscover that. In the meantime, you have a will of your own, a renegade will, you could say, a will that is separate from Thy will, which can act independently and in ignorance of Thy will. And that is allowed.

The Creator is curious to see what will be created when one is detached from or at a distance from the Creator. And so it allows this, all the time knowing that that separate sense of self will one day realize its connection to All That Is. So it allows you to pursue your personal desires, your ego's desires, your ego's drives, fears, and sense of lack. The Creator allows you to respond to life as if you were completely separate and to discover and learn and grow and evolve as a result of this misunderstanding. All the while, it brings you understandings that will correct that misunderstanding. It brings you teachers and teachings — and life, itself, is a teacher that brings about this understanding ultimately.

Prayer is a means of connecting you with the Divine and with your divine self. What is surrendered in prayer is the false self, the ego. When you pray, you must surrender that false sense of self. Prayer *is* a surrendering of this sense of self. It is humbling yourself enough to say, "I don't know what is best. I don't know what to want. I don't know what to do. I don't know how to make my life happen. Show me, help me, teach me. I am open, available, and willing to receive your guidance because I know my own ego is not capable of providing guidance that will make me happy, because I have discovered this."

The challenges in life bring you to a place of surrender, where you are willing to surrender your desires, ideas, beliefs, and feelings to something higher that *does* know how to guide your life. You realize that what has been guiding your life is flawed, undependable, and untrustworthy, and you willingly surrender your belief that you can make your life happen in a certain way.

The challenges in life bring you to a point of surrender. You realize that life is not in your hands but in the hands of something much greater. And so all that is left to do is to state that surrender and ask for help, for alignment, for a true sense of knowing what is right and true for you in any particular moment.

The information you receive after asking is always only good for a particular moment. You ask and you receive what you need for then. New prayers are needed for future moments. When you feel lost, then you pray again, you ask again, you open yourself up and say, "I don't know what is true for me. Help me, guide me, help me to know, help me to understand, help me to heal, help me to serve, help me to create what you want me to create in this life. What is the instrument I am meant to be now, in this moment, on this day?"

All you can ever know is what you are meant to do and experience now, today, in this moment. And so you pray on an ongoing basis: "What now? What do you want for me now? What is Thy will for this instrument now, today? How can I be of service now? How do I need to grow now? What do I need to understand now? What do I need to heal now?"

It is very helpful to ask these questions, because this is a way of realigning yourself. And yet, when you are very present in your life, there's no need to ask, because in Presence, there is a continual listening for the truth, for what's next, for what you are being moved to do now. Presence is alignment with Thy will. It is alignment with yourself as the instrument of Thy will. Whenever you are present, you respond naturally and spontaneously to Thy will.

Prayer is needed whenever you feel off-base, off-kilter, stressed, contracted, or confused, when the ego has caught you up in its mind-stream and caused you to believe something that is a misunderstanding. Then you need to stop and say, "Wait, I don't understand. I don't know what I need to do now. I don't know how I need to be now. Please help me realign to the state of peace and flow and spontaneity." That's what prayer is for.

Prayer is a bridge that takes you from the false self's world of needing to push and hurry and make things happen, and not knowing what you're supposed to make happen, or believing you do know when you don't. Prayer is a bridge that takes you from that state of consciousness to the state of peace and flow and spontaneity, of just knowing what's true and right in that moment to do.

When you are present, there is a natural, spontaneous flow of activity or non-activity. There's no questioning of the activity but just a doing or stopping of doing that naturally occurs, with no thoughts about it: no questioning, no confusion, no alternate opinion about it. Just simple. You find yourself moving, and that moving feels natural, right, simple, uncomplicated—and it's effective. That's when you know you are the instrument you are meant to be and acting in alignment with God.

And you know very well when you are not acting as that instrument. You know very well when you're not in alignment, because it doesn't feel good to be out of alignment. Life feels difficult, confusing upsetting, stressful, and negative emotions are involved. You all know exactly what it feels like to be out of alignment, when the instrument has gone rogue and it's not doing Thy will.

The gentleness of God allows you to have that experience. God allows you to go rogue, to have whatever experience you are having. But God has built into life a sense of stress and discomfort when that is going on, which is meant to be a sign that brings you Home. That discomfort is a signal: "I'm out of alignment. I need to stop. I need to question. I need to pray." So prayer is a means for becoming that instrument of Thy will again.

You don't have to know anything to pray. It's more of a willingness to not know, a surrendering of knowing that allows you to pray. You say, "I don't know. I'm lost. I'm confused." To be able to pray, you have to be humble enough to ask for help.

The ego doesn't like to have to ask for help. The ego doesn't believe it needs help, so it won't ask. Or sometimes the ego believes it's not worthy to receive help, and so it doesn't ask for that reason. Even that can be a reason to not ask for help. Or the ego may have beliefs that help is not available: "This is not a benevolent universe, and there's no one out there listening to my prayer, so why pray?"

That's a common reason why people don't pray. They think of it as childish. But you are to be as little children: open, receptive, in awe of something greater than yourself, connecting to something greater than yourself and knowing that. That's the little child. The child knows the greatness of the universe. The child is in awe of the universe. He or she hasn't figured it out, doesn't believe that he or she has the answers to everything.

The ego believes it has answers or that it *should*. Therefore, it can't or feels it shouldn't ask for any help. But this is a vast, vast universe, a mysterious universe. There is so much you don't know that you just pretend to know. So realize what you don't know, realize how much there is to know that you don't know. Be humble, be like a little child in that humility and ask. Be sure to ask whenever you need help for whatever you need, and it will be given to you.

Know that it will be given to you in one form or another at one time or another. What you really need is always given to you, especially when you ask for it. So ask for things you really need. Ask for wisdom, love, inspiration, creativity, strength, and courage. These are the things you really need to get through life, and these are the things you actually already have.

To ask for them evokes them. It brings them out in you. It makes you realize that you do already have them. Like Dorothy and her red slippers, you have always had everything you've ever needed to live this life, but your ego has kept you from knowing this. So ask, and that allows you to know this again. It allows you to know the truth, to own those red slippers and to use them.

Talking to God

Prayer is talking to God. It's a one-way conversation, or at least you may feel that it is, but it's a very important conversation to have. For one thing, it identifies the issue, the problem, or the need, the thing you feel is missing that makes you unhappy. To pray for help, you need to be aware of something you want to have changed. This awareness is the first step in changing something you'd like changed. So prayer is very important.

To put a prayer into words, you need to be aware of something you want to say. This awareness empowers you to change whatever you'd like to change. It also enables you to get the assistance from other realms to do that. So when you pray, two things are happening: You're asking for assistance from other realms and calling it forth, but very importantly, you are also defining for yourself what you want on a deeper level. What is it that you think you need or want in order to be happy?

It's important that you understand what makes you unhappy and what you *think* you need to be happy. Some of it is really just that: a thought that you need something and not a real need. Other needs that are identified may be very deep and true needs, and that's important to discover as well. So when you talk to God, you discover things about yourself and become aware of things you might not have been aware of.

This God doesn't have to be an imagination of a wise being. It can be anything that you are comfortable with conceiving God as. So don't let the idea that God must be a being, an entity, stop you from praying. Pray to the universe. Pray to the Intelligence. Pray to the forces that be. Pray to whatever it is you conceive of as a helping force, as wisdom, as intelligence, as the power behind the universe.

God is not actually a singular being, as most of you realize anyway. But it is a force, a force for creation. It is also all of life as it is expressed. So it is the force that creates life, and it is life living itself in the many ways that it does. This is God.

So you pray to this force and ask to be aligned with it and ask for help with whatever you think you need help with. When you speak your needs, you will perhaps discover they aren't true needs and that there is something deeper that is more important to pray for. So an evolution can happen when you open yourself up to speaking to God. You discover things about yourself. This is the basis for therapy as well, or the value of friendship and relationship. When you speak things out loud, you learn things about yourself. So it is with talking with God: You learn things about yourself. Things that are unconscious become conscious. Your awareness grows.

Another very valuable thing about prayer is that it is a way of overcoming certain subconscious blocks. When you speak openly and clearly about what you want, you are also addressing your subconscious and saying, "This is what I want. This is my intention." Whatever subconscious beliefs you have that might be interfering with that desire can be overcome by stating an intention to overcome them. Speaking your intention out loud empowers you to overcome any subconscious forces that are working against attaining that intention.

So prayer can be a way of reprogramming the subconscious and helping you move forward. You form an intention, state that intention, and in doing so, create a new pathway. Perhaps you've been following some habit that hasn't been helpful. When you speak an intention to go in another direction than the usual habit, your subconscious mind aligns with that and says, "Okay, let's go in that direction, now that I know what you want. I thought you wanted the other thing."

The same is true of the forces that are assisting you in other dimensions. When they hear of your intention, they come forward and say, "Okay, she's ready to have something new in her life. She's ready for help. She's finally aware that this needs to change, and that tells us she's ready for us to help her change that." So that's what goes on when you pray.

When you speak to God, you can say anything, and this is very important, because in your own life, with other people, you often can't say just anything. Even with yourself, you sometimes feel that it's not right to think something. With God, you can say anything. With God, there is an all-pervading compassion and love that heals, and so you can say anything.

It's good to say what you're moved to say, to get it out in the open, where you can see it. Then you can see if it's true or not. Sometimes you hold back your thoughts instead of examining them, and in holding them back, they persist. So you may have a negative belief, and until it is acknowledged and examined, it won't stop coming up. It won't be healed unless you see it and examine it, and in that examination, see that it isn't true.

However, it's not enough to recognize a negative thought if you still believe it. You have to recognize it and then see that it's untrue, then you can be free of it. But just seeing a negative thought —just witnessing it—is not going to heal it. It will come up again, although witnessing does diminish its strength.

Witnessing a negative thought is better than identifying with it. Identifying with a negative thought would be consciously, clearly believing it and reinforcing it by speaking it. If you want to be free of that thought, you have to go farther than just witnessing it. You have to examine that thought for its validity.

You will always discover that a negative thought is not true, that it's not valid. A true thought would be true under all circumstances and true always, because that is what truth is. Truth is true. So if a thought that makes you feel bad doesn't pass that test, isn't true always and throughout time, then what good is it? It has no useful purpose. It only makes you feel bad. So you can discard it. To move beyond negative beliefs and misunderstandings, you have to really, truly see that they are useless and untrue. When you stop believing them, they will diminish in their power and arise much less frequently.

In speaking out loud to God, you are speaking these thoughts. Doing this is a little like writing in a journal. You can see what's in your mind, what falseness is there. Speak your thoughts to God, listen to yourself, see the falseness and see what is true. You will know when you are speaking truth in a prayer because of how it feels.

Talking to God is a little bit like therapy. You're talking to a wise, accepting, compassionate being, the ultimate being, who is truly loving you unconditionally. This is a powerful experience, as is therapy for many people when it's done properly. It's very powerful to have a compassionate, accepting being witnessing your life, witnessing your thoughts and your expression. Then you can begin to sort out what's true and isn't true, what's real and isn't real, what you want and what you don't really want, what you need and what you don't really need.

Do this as an exercise in emotional health and well-being. Do this for yourself. This is part of a natural clearing process you can engage in every day. Talk to the Beloved, talk to God, and you will never feel alone, for this Beloved is always there listening. You'll begin to experience that more and more, that the Beloved is always there and always listening, always loving you, always caring.

So you develop a relationship with the Beloved, with God. In that relationship is a wholeness. You can receive what you need within yourself from this relationship. And like any relationship, it requires a certain amount of nurturing—time spent and care given—and then it deepens. A relationship with the Divine doesn't happen overnight. It's something you have to nurture over time. But it is time well spent, as this relationship will support you and give you a sense of stability and a sense of wholeness, completeness.

When you express your needs to the Divine and those needs are fulfilled on the deepest levels, sometimes apparently and sometimes less apparently, there's much less need for others to fulfill your needs. There's less need to speak to others about your needs, who sometimes are not that helpful. Human beings can often reinforce negative thoughts and egoic ways of thinking about things.

You won't find that when you are talking to God. You have an open line, where you talk and listen to yourself, and then you do receive from the Divine as you open up. You receive in various ways. Sometimes those ways are fairly tangible and measurable. Other times, they are immeasurable, and yet, you've received something.

You can't evaluate what you receive in these conversations in the usual way. You can't say, "Well, I asked God to fix my problem, and it didn't get fixed, so what's the use?" There is something much deeper that goes on in prayer than asking for something and seeing if you get it. There is engagement on a much deeper and more important level, a level that relates to your growth and evolution, your healing and your deepening.

Your spiritual growth is not easily assessed by your mind. When you open up to the Divine in this way, it is about your spiritual growth. You're opening up for help on the level of your growth, your evolution, your healing, and that is what you'll receive help with. You may receive help in the mundane aspects of life as well. Who knows? But that is not the purpose of prayer.

The purpose of prayer is not to get things from God. That is not what prayer is about. Prayer is a discovery of your own inner self: where you are at, where you are going, and how you will get there. These are the things that are discovered in prayer by speaking and listening to yourself and also by listening inwardly to whatever answers you might receive.

Just as important as speaking to God is listening to God. When you listen to God, you listen with your whole self. You're not listening with your ears, because it's not that you're going to receive words, most likely, in answer to any questions you have. But your Heart will receive answers. Your body will receive answers. You will receive knowings, a sense of rightness, courage, strength, inspiration, and ideas.

When you open up this line of communication with God, you open yourself up to more of what has already been given to you to help you along your way. The beings that are guiding your life can activate your strength and courage. They can drop an inspiration or idea into your body or mind. They can steer you here or there with feelings of excitement and joy. These are the answers you receive when you develop a relationship to God in prayer.

You may not receive these "answers" as soon as you ask for them, though. They are scattered throughout your day. You never know when you might receive an answer. All of a sudden you have an answer or an inspiration. All of a sudden you have an idea, you feel strength, you feel excitement, you feel joy, or you feel connected. These are the answers to your prayers. Life brings you the people you need, the opportunities you need, and the ideas and inspiration you need.

Life brings you everything you need — and nothing more. You aren't brought things you don't need. That could be confusing and throw you off-track. Other people might bring you opportunities, but if they aren't in alignment with your greatest good, they probably won't work out or you probably won't feel like pursuing them. So if life brings you an opportunity and you are joyful and excited about it, then by all means, say yes to it because it must be right. Opportunities are answers to your prayers, whether or not you recognize them as answers.

When you pray, you always receive something, but if you don't notice what you are receiving, it's as if you haven't received it. For instance, if you receive strength, and you don't recognize the strength inside yourself, it's as if you don't have it. Or if you recognize the strength and talk yourself out of it, it's as if it hasn't been given to you.

It's important to recognize these gifts or you won't use them. You won't feel that you have them. You'll close down and think you don't have the support you need, and the egoic fears will take over. You have to work at noticing and acknowledging the subtle gifts that are available to you and also the opportunities that are not so subtle.

It doesn't come naturally to acknowledge these things because the mind does not acknowledge subtle realities, such as courage, faith, love, strength, and patience. The egoic mind doesn't view these as significant. It sees the world from a place of lack. Even when you have been given gifts, the egoic mind often doesn't see them or accept them or utilize them. It sees right past them and goes on thinking that there isn't enough, that this is a limited universe, that "I never get what I want. I can't seem to get what I need. The world is against me." This is the egoic perception. It's your programming to feel lacking inside and to feel that the world is lacking, unkind, unsupportive, threatening, and that you have to fight to survive.

These beliefs, themselves, create this reality. Believing that the world is a fearful place and that goodness is not behind life, but difficulty and perhaps even evil, will create that very experience. These beliefs become a self-fulfilling prophecy. The mind creates its own reality by believing certain things. You become your own worst enemy when you believe your thoughts.

The thoughts in your thought-stream are not your friend. They don't have your best interest at heart. They don't give you courage or strength or patience— they do the opposite, don't they? The thoughts in your head take away your courage, your strength, and your patience. They make you irritable, impatient, unhappy, and feeling like a victim. How are these thoughts your friend? How are they helpful? Why do you listen to them?

And so you have to learn to listen on more subtle levels to the gifts that appear on subtle levels. You have to learn to notice the courage, the strength, the patience, the perseverance, and all the other qualities you innately have by virtue of being a divine being: "As above, so below."

The Divine is goodness, and you have this goodness within you. This goodness is not so accessible at times because your egoic mind is your default. The egoic mind takes away these gifts. It neutralizes them. It disempowers you. So you have to learn to move beyond the mind to regain your power as a divine son or daughter. You have all the goodness, all the strength, and everything you need to live this life beautifully, happily, joyfully, and to be in service to all of creation in the way you are meant to be. You have everything you need to be this in the world. You have to overcome the egoic mind, though, which interferes with you knowing this and tapping into these gifts from God, which are qualities of your divine nature.

So the key is to notice the gifts: Notice the courage, notice the love, notice the patience, notice the strength and the abilities to persevere, to care, and to connect with others. Everything that is good about human beings is your divine nature. So, dear ones, notice how wonderful you are. Notice your goodness, notice your strength, and know that they are gifts given to you to help you on your way and to help you live the life you are meant to live. These are your resources.

You have not been left alone and you are not lacking in any way. You always have whatever you need. So know this and know that when you pray, that will help you receive what you need and help you notice that you have received it, because once you ask for something, you'll be looking to receive it. So prayer helps you to notice what you're receiving and *that* you're receiving on a continual basis.

Developing a Relationship with God

Developing a relationship with the Divine is important because then you will not feel alone. The ego causes you to feel alone and lost in this vast universe, and it undermines any connections that you do make. It undermines love. Developing a relationship with God is the primary relationship, the most important relationship.

You can't have a relationship with God unless you are able to experience God as good and trustworthy. That's usually what prevents people from having a relationship with God. They feel that life is not good and God is not good, that life is not trustworthy and God is not trustworthy. How can you have a relationship with someone or something you don't believe is trustworthy? Your ideas about God can interfere with having a relationship with God. So some of your ideas about God need to change.

God is good. God is supportive. God is here for your benefit. Life *is* supporting you. It always has, sometimes in miraculous ways but in the most mundane ways as well: providing you with the air you breathe, the ground you stand on, the people and the help you need, the food you need. Life provides for your basic needs.

And, yes, you can find examples where people are starving, and you may ask, "How is that providing for their needs?" The divine being that you are wishes to have every manner of experience, and so each of you has had lifetimes in which you experienced the most devastating conditions. Even these conditions serve to help you grow in certain ways. They develop patience and compassion and sensitivity. They serve a purpose in the evolution of life.

In the end, you have far more lifetimes of abundance and happiness than you ever have of disease and unhappiness. You are an eternal soul, and the lifetimes you have had that have been difficult are small in number compared to the countless, in fact, infinite lives you will have and have had throughout time, including on other planets.

This third dimension of earth is like a school, and it is a difficult school sometimes. But it is a school you eventually graduate from and never have to go back to, unless you choose to for the challenge, which some of you do, because after graduating from third dimension, you know you have the strength and courage to overcome anything the third dimension could throw at you.

From the perspective of all of your lifetimes, from the perspective of infinity, the difficult lifetimes are inconsequential; and yet, they are also some of the most important lifetimes you'll ever experience in terms of your evolution. So very much is learned— much more than you realize during that lifetime, for much of the learning isn't realized until after that lifetime. And then it's brought into the next lifetime and lifetimes. What you have learned is like a jewel you've earned that makes you a better person forevermore. So life is good, even when it's hard.

You must trust that life is good, and then you will begin to see that it is. Once you have some trust, you can begin to have a deeper relationship with God. That will fill you and fulfill you, because the acceptance and love of God can be felt by you the closer this relationship becomes. So the only difficult part of having a relationship with God is in the beginning when it's difficult to get it started because of a lack of trust due to mistaken beliefs and misunderstandings about God.

These beliefs must be examined. You must look at your ideas about God. You need to understand the truth about God and not believe the lies. Anything that makes you unhappy or frightened is a lie. If goodness is behind life—and it is—then nothing about God could make you unhappy. Goodness is love, goodness is joy, goodness is peace. Only goodness can come from God, from knowing the truth about God. The opposite is also true: When you believe something false about God, you're left feeling bad and scared and unhappy.

This is the ego's natural state. It lives in fear and a sense of lack and separation. This is not the truth. The mind has made it up that you are lacking. The mind has made it up that life is fearful. This is what you have to see through. It is a very clever illusion, and it catches people up for many, many lifetimes until, one day, they begin to see through it. They begin to see that they've been told lies. All along, their egoic mind, the voice in their head, has been telling them lies about life, about themselves, about others, and about God.

When you start seeing the truth, life changes. You experience life differently, and that means you behave differently. You express goodness, you express love, and you express peace, and that creates more of the same. This is one of the lessons you are here to learn: What you put out comes back to you. Negative thoughts and beliefs cause you to put out negativity, and then you get back negativity and unhappiness, without realizing that you created that unhappiness by believing negative thoughts and expressing them.

When you change your thoughts, you change your life, because you change your experience of life. When you start seeing God as good and life as good, supportive, kind, wonderful, and miraculous, then it becomes so. If you believe that life is supportive, you will act as if it is. You will notice how it is. You will be able to acknowledge that it is supportive. You will tell others. You will become a teacher and say, "Look, look, life is good."

That is my message. Life is good, and once you know that, you can have a deeper and closer relationship with God. And that changes everything, because you know you're not alone. You know you are connected, and with this connection comes great power, great support, and great love. You are full instead of empty. You're not lacking anymore. And when you're not lacking, you overflow, and when you overflow, you attract love, peace, and abundance to you.

Know that you are children of a very wealthy, loving, and perfectly wise Father/Mother. That is your inheritance. Your inheritance is everything you need — and more. Once you realize you have more than you need, you start giving that out. When you give that out, your life changes, because the more you give, the more you get back. That is a natural law. It has to be.

Knowing that you are the child of an abundant Father/Mother allows you to be generous. This generosity creates the very world that you are meant to have, that you are meant to experience, that you are meant to create. You are not a pauper. You are not alone. You are not unsupported. Your life is perfectly unfolding as it is meant to. You are co-creating with God. You are partners with God. You *are* God. You are an extension of God.

From the standpoint of God, this life is a marvelous experience. God relishes being in third dimension as you. God loves creation. God loves you as a co-creator. God loves life. God loves life through you. When you are connected to God and have a relationship with God, you feel this love for life. You experience it at your core. You look out of your eyes and see beauty and the magnificence of this creation, not lack or imperfection. It's all perfect just as it is. It's beautiful. It's wonderful.

There's no other place, no other moment, and no other being like you. This creation is unique, and God relishes it, savors it, enjoys it, and loves it, for soon it will change into something new and different, and God loves that too. God loves the change, the newness. Where is the flow going next? How will these creations act? What will they create? What will they do next? What fun! What joy!

Such gratitude there is in the heart of God and in you. When you turn and look and notice what is here inside you on a subtle level, on the deepest of levels, you will feel so full. The gratitude, the peace, the love, the awe, the wonderment of God is within you, and it makes you strong and puts everything in perspective so that nothing can bother you. You have all the strength you need to deal with any difficulty. From this place of power, you are love, you are the Creator, and you've come Home, as you were meant to.

That's what this is all about. In the third dimension, you are learning to come home to God. You're learning who you really are, and that takes many, many lifetimes. But eventually, finally, you do see the truth. You realize: "I'm divine! I *am* God. I am the expression of a benevolent God, and no harm can come to me." Once you know that on the deepest level and you know it fully in every moment, you are ready to graduate third dimension. Then you will continue to evolve and grow in greater love and greater co-creation with God in other dimensions.

But for now, this is how it is in this dimension — you have an ego that makes it difficult to see the truth and have a relationship with God. You have to work at it. You have to spend time talking with God, trusting in the goodness of God, regardless of what your egoic mind and others say about life, regardless of the fears that come up, regardless of the bad behavior of others.

You have to learn to trust life, and then your life will change. Then you will begin to experience the truth about life, the great good news: You are one with the Creator, you have always been one with the Creator, and you are here to create, to be happy, to learn, to grow, to love, and to serve. Developing a relationship with God by speaking with God, by acknowledging the presence of God in your life, and by noticing the gifts you are given will help you live the life you are meant to live.

CHAPTER 3
Gratitude

Gratitude is so important to your happiness that it deserves an entire chapter, not that there is so much to say about it, but what there is to say about it is important. Gratitude is important to your well-being and the well-being of everyone around you, because how you feel inside is transmitted to others, and they transmit that to others. Each of you is like a little broadcasting station. You broadcast your state of consciousness to others. Whether you are aware of it or not, that is going on in every moment. If you are unhappy, you broadcast unhappiness. If you are happy, you broadcast happiness.

Your personal happiness is not a selfish endeavor. It is very important that you maintain a state of consciousness that is positive, which is another way of saying "happy," because this affects not only you, but everyone else. This is how the world is uplifted: one person at a time. You uplift others by uplifting yourself. So gratitude and all of the other practices you do to become happier and more aligned with your true self are not in the least bit selfish but quite the opposite. When you align yourself with the ego, it's a very selfish, self-centered, and unhappy place. This doesn't do anyone any good. It is your responsibility to take care of your emotional health and well-being by learning to be happy.

One of the ways you can become happy is through a practice of gratitude. I say "practice" because acknowledging gratitude is often something that has to be done again and again, since your default state as a human being is to not be grateful. The egoic state of consciousness is the opposite of grateful. It doesn't see abundance but lack, and how can you be grateful for lack?

You have to train yourself to see abundance, and gratitude is a way to do that, to see what is real, actually, because what is real *is* abundant. What is real is bountiful, benevolent, and good. So you have to train yourself to see that instead of seeing life as the ego sees it. That is the work of transforming consciousness — to recognize that the egoic state of consciousness is not your true state and does not reflect reality. It reflects the ego's perceptions of reality, which are misperceptions and misunderstandings. The ego believes there isn't enough, and it believes *it* isn't enough, so it must strive and struggle against everyone else to get what it wants.

The opposite is true: Reality is not a zero-sum game. Reality is abundant and works very well when you realize that you are working together with everyone and everything in the universe to evolve and provide for each other. Life is not about fighting to get your share; it is more a matter of finding your place in the universe and doing that. When you do that, you will experience the support you need. That support might not always look the way the ego wants it to, but it will be the support you need to continue to evolve and serve in the way you came here to serve.

Service is a big part of this game called life. When you serve others, you are serving yourself. That is one of the lessons you are learning. You are learning that service to others and giving to others is how you support yourself, how you keep the wheels of life turning in your favor. When you listen to the ego, the wheels get stuck. They can't move. You stop evolving or end up fighting the evolutionary process. You can't really stop evolving, but you can slow your evolution down significantly. When you listen to the egoic mind, you slow it down.

You have to find a different way of seeing and moving through life, and then you will be aligned with your own evolution and that of the Whole. That alignment will bring you everything you need. It's not up to you what's brought to you. There's something much greater that brings what you need to you, and it knows exactly what you need. This is Grace. Grace does the heavy lifting for you. It does the work for you, but you have to be aligned with Grace for it to work for you.

To be aligned with Grace, you can't be listening to your egoic mind, because that is the aspect of yourself that is generally out of alignment with Grace. The only thing that interferes with your alignment, with the hand of Grace that is moving your evolution along and supplying you with everything you need, is the egoic mind—your very own mind, which you rely on and believe in so dearly.

How ironic it is that the voice in your head seems so real and so true when, in fact, it is the only thing here that is not so real. Of course, thought has its own type of reality. However, thought creates a virtual reality that takes you away from reality, away from alignment with Thy will and with what Thy will has in store for you, with what it wants for you, with the life you are meant to live. Gratitude is one of the most valuable tools you have for realigning with Thy will, with the deeper self.

Gratitude is valuable, in part, because it is so simple and so accessible. It doesn't cost a thing to feel grateful, and it barely takes a moment. If you experience gratitude often enough, it becomes your perception, your reality. That is the goal, for this state of gratitude to be your ongoing reality instead of the state of lack, which is the ego's reality.

You are blessed to have this alternative. You aren't meant to suffer and stay in the egoic state of consciousness. You are meant to find methods to help you get out of this state of consciousness — because once you are outside of it, you experience the truth, which is that reality is good. It's wonderful, and it's possible to be happy within this world. Yes, there is so much struggle and strife in the world, and there will always be challenges, but even so, it is possible to be happy. You must learn to shift from the ego's perspective to a truer one, and gratitude will help you do that.

The practice of gratitude is the very simple act of noticing what you are grateful for. When I say "you," I mean the true you, which can be experienced in any moment. You only have to look and see what your being is seeing and experiencing and what *it* is grateful for in that moment. There is an underlying sense of gratitude in every moment, and you can learn to tune in to that stream of gratitude and bring it to the forefront. When you are in the egoic state of consciousness, this gratitude is in the background, but you can bring it forward with just a little bit of application of your will.

You can choose to be grateful. This is one thing everyone can do. You can make this choice, and you need to make this choice whenever you are feeling ungrateful. If you're feeling ungrateful, lacking, unhappy, or discontent, then that's the time to apply this practice of gratitude. Look around and notice what there is to be grateful for. Start with your physical surroundings, by just looking around you for what you are grateful for.

There is always something to be grateful for in your surroundings. There is always a sky. There is always ground holding you up. Usually, there's much, much more than that. But if you start with basic things, such as the sky and the ground supporting you, that opens you up to noticing what else you are grateful for. The more you look, the more you discover that there is a great deal to be grateful for.

But you have to stop—stop thinking. Stop and just be. Be quiet and just look. This looking for what you are grateful for has to come from a place of quiet. It can't be the egoic mind looking, because it sees lack. So you have to stop being involved with what your egoic mind is telling you and just notice what your eyes actually see.

Notice the beauty, the colors, the textures. Notice the light, the sparkle. Notice the miraculous bugs. Notice the micro-world, which is so amazing—the detail. Notice the vastness of the sky and the stars.

Then you can notice physical sensations: Notice the breeze or the air against your skin. Notice the sun, the warmth. Notice the blood pumping through your body. What a miracle that is!

Notice how beautifully your body holds you up. Notice how beautifully your body delivers sensory input. What a miracle that is—this body that you have! How grateful you can be to have a body that can experience life, that can see, feel, and smell.

You may also turn your attention to sounds. What sounds might you be grateful for? There are so many. All kinds of sounds: manmade sounds and nature sounds. All amazing. Everything that is manmade—what a miracle! Cars that travel on roads—what a miracle! And bees, birds, and wind rustling through the trees. How beautiful! They are nothing but perfect.

This is the experience of your being. Your being is in awe of life. It is in great wonderment at this beautiful, beautiful world. So you must learn to see with eyes that experience life as the wonder that it is.

Then you can begin to experience gratitude for things in your personal life. You can be grateful for your dog, your cat, your friends, your partner, all of the beings that help you along your way. Can you make a list of them? Who are the people who have given you a hand, whom you have loved, whom you have helped? It is a miracle that they come into your life. So much helping going on. Can you focus on that, on all the help you've received from others, on all the love you've received from others rather than on problems?

The mind sees problems with people. It wants more from people. But you're always getting exactly what you need—not always what you want, but what you need. And you can be grateful for that. There isn't a person in this world who isn't receiving, every single day of their life, gifts from other people, gifts from life. Can you notice them? Can you name them? Can you focus on them?

This will make you happy, when you focus on what is given to you and what is good about your life and about your day. It is a wonderful practice to list the things each day that you are grateful for. You'll have to think hard to find them at first. Then after you do this exercise a few more times, it will be easy for you to list them. They will come to you like a flood.

That's what you want to experience, an ease with naming what you're grateful for, because that means you'll easily feel grateful during your day. But first it's helpful to name the things that you are grateful for.

That gets the flow moving, and then the feelings of gratitude can begin to flow. The more you do that, the more that becomes how you regularly feel.

This is the work. It's not that hard. Just notice, from your being, what you are grateful for. Notice how your being is feeling and what it is grateful for. Write things down. Make it an exercise, like a game. What is there to be grateful for in *this* moment? And now in this moment, what is there to be grateful for?

This is a good use of the mind. You're using it as a tool to discover what you are grateful for. You're using it instead of it using you by showing you a world of lack. Don't buy into that. This is not a world of lack. This is a world of great bounty. Look how many billions of people it has supported, not to mention insects, animals, trees, fish — every beautiful lifeform on this planet. Billions of lifeforms, including microbes and all sorts of forms of life you can't even see and don't even know about, are being supported by this biosphere. Beautiful.

You are an integral part of it. You and every being is meant to be here. You belong here. Human beings are the most blessed species on the planet because you have free will and the capacity to manipulate your environment and create, like no other species on this planet. And you can be grateful for that. How wonderful it is to create, to choose and see the results of your choices.

And to simply exist! There is great pleasure and enjoyment in simply existing, if you turn your attention to what your being is experiencing. There is gratitude in simply existing and experiencing life. You can always be grateful for that.

You can also be grateful for all that you learn, for the evolution and growth that happens to every one of you. You couldn't possibly be alive and not grow and evolve. Sometimes you interfere with this growth and slow it down, but it's impossible for you to *not* grow toward greater goodness, greater intelligence, and greater capacities, strengths, and talents. You evolve in so many ways. What a joy that is. Can you experience your being rejoicing in that and being grateful for that?

Your being loves to grow. It loves to experience. It even loves to experience the negative results of your choices because that is how it grows. Your ego might not like those results, however. "Negative" is, in fact, a concept the ego applies to experience. There is no such thing as negative. This good/bad judgment on the part of the ego is not the perception of your being. It is all good to this being that you are.

When you come into alignment with the being that you are, you experience all life as good: the challenges, the growth, and the disappointments.

What fun! Your being experiences all of it as fun. Challenges — yes! Growth — yes! It says yes to all of it. It loves all of it. It is grateful for all of it, because when you are an eternal being, you love all experience, any experience. Nothing can destroy you, nothing can hurt you. You are an eternal being. That's who you really are. This eternal being embraces and loves every aspect of life, not just the so-called good experiences. It's grateful for all of it. It loves.

The reason your being loves is because the Creator *is* love. There is nothing else here but love, so naturally that is the ground of your being. That is the essential experience of your being — it is one of love. How grateful you can be that this universe, this creation, is based on love and goodness. And how grateful you can be that you are eternal, for after this relatively brief lifetime in third dimension, you will leave your body and take on a new form, perhaps another third dimensional body or perhaps a fourth dimensional body, and then you'll go around again and experience life again.

So let this be the lifetime when you decide that you can be happy, when you decide to be grateful for this life and love this life from the depths of your being by aligning with the love for life that is already here. You don't have to create that love for life. You don't have to make it happen. You don't have to struggle to discover it. All you have to do is turn your attention to the subtle experience of gratitude that your being is already and always having. Turn your attention away from thought onto the very subtle realm of your being.

The subtle realm is a realm of energy. Gratitude, love, and peace — all of these qualities, or experiences, of your being are experienced on a subtle, energetic level. The subtle realm is more difficult to perceive than the mental realm. You have to train yourself to notice this more subtle realm. That's all. It's a matter of noticing it and keeping your attention on the subtle realm long enough so that you can experience it.

Whatever you put your attention on is magnified in your experience and becomes your experience, your reality. So when you go looking for the subtle experience of gratitude or love or peace, if you can find even the slightest sense of it and focus on that and stay with that, you'll begin to experience it more strongly. That's all it takes.

Do you have the will to make that choice? That might not be up to you. The will to make that choice is developed with spiritual progress. But you can at least not interfere with the spiritual progress that wants to come about. If you are reading this, then it may be time for you to make that choice more frequently.

Choose gratitude, choose happiness, choose love, peace, kindness, and compassion. You have to use a little bit of your will. Instead of following the path of least resistance, use your will to make another choice. You are waking up from the path of least resistance, which is following the egoic mind. That is what awakening is about. You are waking up out of the programmed sense of yourself as a limited, fearful, and lacking individual. You're waking up out of the thought-stream and realizing who you really are.

So some effort needs to be made. That effort is in the form of choice. You make a choice. In a particular moment, will you dive into your thoughts and believe them and suffer more, or will you take a step back from them and look at them and say: "No, not this time. I'm not going there. I'm going to turn my attention to what is real. What am I grateful for now? What is here now in this moment?"

Presence is in this present moment. Presence is grateful, loving, kind, compassionate, and happy. Be present. Be here now in this beautiful moment. Notice the beauty of this moment. Noticing the beauty of this moment and noticing what you are grateful for will bring you into this present moment and into Presence.

Choosing to be grateful is a bridge into Presence, which is an experience of enhanced gratitude and love. So first you may have to fabricate some gratitude, drum it up: imagine what you are grateful for, make a list, look for it. At first you have to put a little effort into it, but doing so will bring you into Presence, where gratitude lives. Doing these exercises in gratitude brings you into the place of true gratitude.

The more you experience the place of true gratitude, the more that becomes your reality. Then the easier it is to evoke gratitude. The enlightened mind is a grateful mind, which is where everyone is headed. You are all headed toward enlightenment. Gratitude will help you get there, and it will be a wonderful companion along the way. No matter how long it takes for you to become fully enlightened, gratitude can be your companion. It will speed your way and make your way much happier.

CHAPTER 4
Surrender

Surrender usually has a negative connotation. It often means giving up something you dearly love. But spiritual surrender is very different from that. It's quite the opposite, actually. Spiritual surrender brings you everything you have ever wanted. Instead of taking something away, you are given something very precious. You are given peace of mind, you are given a loving heart and a gracious way of being, and you are given happiness and contentment. Isn't that what everyone really wants? Contentment? Don't you just want to be satisfied once and for all? Don't you just want to stop wanting, stop feeling that you need something, stop feeling that you are lacking?

What you surrender in spiritual surrender is this sense of lack, the sense of longing and wanting and needing something that you can't have. That sense of lack and those desires are created by the egoic mind, the voice in your head. It says: "I need this, I want this,

I have to have this." This voice is the source of suffering, not the fact that you don't have something, but the fact that you want something you don't have.

Wanting something you don't have is suffering. And wanting something you don't have is just a thought. The desire to have something comes from a thought: that you want it, that you need it, that you have to have it. And then the feeling of longing, sadness, and desire are created—from a thought. Without this thought, where would you be? You would be without desire and without longing and suffering.

It is your nature as human beings to think these thoughts and have these desires and suffer over them. But you are here to discover your divine nature, which does not suffer, which does not have such thoughts, which is already full, complete, and content with life just as it is.

Your divine nature is content with this ever-changing river of life, which is always bringing something new to you. The mind doesn't see it that way, however. The mind doesn't see that there is a river here. It believes it has to make life happen, and the way it makes life happen is by thinking about it—about what it needs, what it wants, and what will make it happy—and then going after those things. That is how life is created on the level of the ego.

SURRENDER   81

That's fine. You are meant to be human and to
have these desires and thoughts until a certain time in
your evolution, when you are done with the suffering,
and you begin to look for the cause of your suffering,
and you turn and look at these thoughts. Other
spiritual teachers and masters have pointed to this: The
cause of suffering is your desires, your thoughts. But it
is only at a certain point in your evolution that you are
ready to see the truth about that. So until you are ready
to see the truth, it's fine that you have your desires and
follow them.

There have always been deeper desires driving
you, which are designed to fulfill your particular life
purpose. These are quite different than the thoughts in
your mind of "I want" and "I need" and "I have to
have." The deeper desires come from a place that is
wordless. They arrive and are experienced as urges,
drives, motivation, ah-has, excitement, joy, and
energy. These deeper desires are meant to be fulfilled
by you and can hardly not be fulfilled by you, because
there is a certain compelling nature to them.

However, sometimes these deeper desires are at
odds with the voice in your head. That's when it is
most important to attend to the desires of the Heart
rather than the desires of the mind. The desires of the
Heart, of the deepest self, will make you happy in a
way that the desires of your egoic mind never will.

If you give up the desires of the egoic mind, that is, if you don't listen to them and don't follow them, then what you are left with are the desires of the deeper self, the true self, the divine self. These are the desires that arise moment to moment and compel you and impel you to move in certain directions: Suddenly you feel moved to do something. Suddenly you think of something that inspires you. Suddenly you are excited and energized to create something. This is how the deeper desires manifest within you, not as thoughts, but as spontaneous urges in the moment. Who knows where those urges will lead? They are going somewhere, and you can trust that they'll take you in the direction you need to go.

Because the desires of the deeper self are sometimes at odds with the egoic self, it is sometimes necessary to give up the ego's desires in deference to something that is more important, meaningful, and fulfilling. That is what surrender is about. Surrender is a giving up of the ego's desires in deference to deeper desires, the ones that will make you truly happy. There is a need to surrender certain thoughts that can get in the way of fulfilling your deeper desires.

Thoughts are what is surrendered in spiritual surrender. You surrender thoughts about what you think you want and what you think you need to be happy. You surrender these thoughts, knowing that once you do, you will actually be happy, because that will allow you to be in touch with the deeper movements within your being that will bring you happiness.

Your egoic mind doesn't know what will make you happy. It pretends to know. It *thinks* it knows, but it doesn't actually know. The voice in your head is just programming that is coming up in your mind, and everyone has similar programming. The egoic mind wants power, comfort, safety, security, status, and privilege. But these things have never made anyone happy. The source of happiness is not more power, more money, or more material things.

It is difficult to see that in this world. It seems that these things would make you happy. And when you first get them, they do create a sense of happiness. But that happiness doesn't last. It can't. The mind is always creating new desires and demands on life in order to be happy.

Fortunately, happiness is here already. It's part of your true nature to be happy. The being that you are is happy — happy to be alive, to exist, to experience, to create, to solve problems, to learn, to grow, and to love. That is what life is, really — all of those things. This is what you are here to do, and when you do these things, you're happy.

You might be wondering what you would do without desires. It's hard to imagine a life without following your desires. What would that look like? The truth is, you would be following the urges and spontaneous movements in the moment that bring about your life and actually have always been bringing about your life. Your life is unfolding with or without the involvement of your egoic mind. The ego pretends that it is making your life happen, but in fact, life is happening on its own. Moment to moment, life is bringing you new things and causing you to move in certain directions and take certain actions and speak. Life is happening through you already, and it always has been.

But the mind pretends that it is doing it all — that it has to do it all and that it is making life happen. The mind assumes that if you didn't follow your desires and thoughts, you would sit like a bump on a log, doing nothing. And, of course, that's ridiculous. No one could ever just sit and do nothing. That would be impossible. There would always be movement coming from the life within you that would cause you to take action in certain directions.

The life that is living you is moving you moment to moment. Just notice how it's doing that without any thought. So much of what you do during your day is activity that is done without thought. Then there is all the activity that is accompanied by thought. But still, the body moves, the body breathes, the body takes care of what it needs to take care of. It knows how to do those things.

There is an intelligence, there is life within this body, and it is only partially governed by your egoic mind. It is, you could say, more governed by the cells themselves than by the egoic mind. This life that you are is so intelligent; it knows exactly how to stay alive, to be alive, and to prosper.

It is your egoic mind that takes away some of this prosperity, this life, this happiness, this natural contentment. It is the egoic mind that is discontent. The thoughts in your head are discontent. Life, itself, is not flawed. It's not problematic, but the mind makes it so. The mind sees things as problems, but problems are a concept created by the mind.

This life that is living you does not know problems. Your being just moves and responds naturally to life. Programmed deep within your being is a certain agenda, a life plan. This plan is unfolded by your being in cooperation with other beings who are guiding you, and it is all done nonverbally, without thought.

The enlightened mind is a mind that has so much light in it that the egoic mind is no longer influencing the body-mind. There is just a comfortable flow from one activity to the next, a knowing what to say and not say, a quiet contentment and peace with life, an open-hearted love of life, and an awe of life. That is your natural state. The mind itself doesn't become enlightened; it just becomes so full of light that there's no room for thought.

So what is surrendered and what needs to be surrendered are just thoughts — desires and thoughts about "I," which create the false self. All of your thoughts about "I" can be surrendered. You can give them up. You don't need them anymore. At a certain point in your evolution, you see this: "Oh, I'm not the 'I' that I think I am! I'm the life force that is moving this body-mind without thought." What a revelation this is when you see this.

Other thoughts you have to be willing to surrender are thoughts about the past. These thoughts are critical to your identity, that is, the identity of the false self. You — who you think you are — is to a large extent an accumulation of what you've thought about yourself in the past as a result of your experiences.

Thoughts about the past come up in your mind as "I" thoughts: "I did this," "I am this," "I have this," "I like this." This sense of "I," which we call the false self, is created by thoughts about yourself. All of these thoughts about yourself are thoughts you've had in the past about yourself.

Nearly every "I" thought you have is a thought about an idea about yourself in the past or an idea that was formed because of some past experience. Then this idea gets projected into a future thought about yourself: "I will be this way," "I have to have this," "I want this." There is a running story about you going on in your mind: "This happened to me, and now I'm this way, and so this is what I need in the future."

Thoughts about the past, however, are just that—thoughts. The past no longer exists, nor does this "you" in the past. It is an idea of yourself in the past, a memory or an image that's been created and held by your mind, as if it's real. And it's not.

This wouldn't be a problem if the false self didn't prevent you from experiencing your true self—because you can't really be identified with your false self and also be deeply experiencing your true self at the same time. You are either experiencing one or the other, although your true self is always in the background, always available to be experienced. Your true self never goes away, but if you are focusing on ideas about yourself, you aren't going to be experiencing life in the here and now.

What is experiencing life in the here and now is not really a self. It's the experience of life, but there is no separate self that is having this experience. So when I say "true self," I don't really mean that there is an individual self that you could identify in any kind of way as short or tall or this way or that way.

This true self is actually *what* is experiencing your life, and this "what" is very mysterious. It is not a thing; it is simply the experience of whatever is being experienced. So when you drop out of thoughts about yourself, what you are left with is an experience of life, which is the true sense of life, unadulterated and uncolored by thoughts or feelings about life. The being that you are is aptly called a "being." It is more like a verb and an experiencing than a thing.

Are you willing to give up your thoughts about the past? One thing that would help you do this is to see that thoughts about your past don't serve you as you might think they do. You might think it is useful to think about your past, that it somehow helps you function better in the present. But if you really look at that idea, you see that it is false. Your thoughts about the past don't help you function in the here and now.

You have certain conditioning built into your being that does help you function in the here and now: You don't run into doors. You manage to stay upright when you need to. The conditioning you need to function is already in the cells of your body. It is already known by you. You don't need to think about the past to not bump into walls.

Being in the present moment is simple and automatic. There is an ease about it. On the other hand, thoughts about the past and future, thoughts about yourself, and about your beliefs, opinions, and desires interfere with your functioning in the here and now. You actually don't need these thoughts to function. They clutter up this simple moment with unnecessary mental activity.

And yet, these thoughts seem so important, so necessary. That's the illusion. The illusion is that the thoughts that run through your mind, which belong to the voice in your head, are functional, necessary, important, and true. That simply isn't true. Once you see that deeply, it will change your life, because that realization allows you to be present in the here and now without the clutter of thoughts.

From that place of peace, you are able to function much better. But more importantly, you are in contact with the deepest self and all of its qualities, such as love, peace, contentment, compassion, and of course wisdom. This is where your wisdom comes from. It comes from deep within you, not from your thoughts. Your wisdom is deep in your bones, and it arrives also in the form of intuitions. So all of the conditioning you need is already embedded in you, and all of the wisdom you need to function and be happy and live the life you are meant to live is available to you moment to moment when it is needed.

So dear ones, please understand that you give up nothing when you give up the thoughts about yourself and the thoughts about the past. All you are giving up when you surrender are thoughts. That is all that needs to be surrendered in spiritual surrender.

But that is easier said than done because the human being is in love with thoughts. Human beings are fascinated by thoughts and attached to thoughts, desires, and the sense of self. Even if the sense of self is a negative sense of self, there is an attachment to this "I." This attachment is built into the human being.

The attachment to "I" and to every other thought is what is broken when you become awakened and enlightened. You can drop this attachment when you see that you are something much greater than this "I" and that the desires in the thought-stream have never served you.

So you are not giving up something for nothing. You are surrendering what is in the way of experiencing your true nature and what might interfere with fulfilling your life purpose and with fulfilling the deeper desires that are meant to unfold your life plan. You do not lose anything in spiritual surrender. You only gain. You gain everything.

But first you have to see that there is something else here besides this imaginary "I" that you think you are and its desires. You have to begin to realize that you are something much greater. This is realized when you drop out of your thoughts and into the present moment.

Being very present in the moment is an experience of realization of your true self—if you stay there long enough. If you only stay there briefly, you won't really experience the alternative to the false self. You won't really experience your deeper self. You have to drop more deeply into the present moment to experience who you really are.

That means you have to not think your thoughts about yourself for more than just a few seconds. Can you do that? Can you *not* be absorbed in your thoughts about yourself for more than a few seconds? Can you do it for a minute? Can you do it for many minutes?

All of you get lost in the present moment when you are doing something you love and when you are having fun or when you are very focused. You all know what it is like to lose your thoughts about yourself and to just fall into the present moment. You fall into a love for life for however long you are not thinking.

The key to happiness is to fall out of love with your thoughts. Then you will naturally be in love with life. You fall out of love with your thoughts by seeing the truth about them, by seeing that you don't need them. But this is a Catch-22, because you won't really know that you don't need your thoughts unless you spend some time without them.

That is what meditation is for. Meditation is a means of experiencing what it's like to be aligned with your deeper self for longer and longer periods of time. Then you will begin to feel that this deeper self is real. It takes on more reality: You real-ize it. When that realization is deep enough, you will no longer be so attached to the thoughts in your head, and you'll be able to see them clearly for what they are. The thoughts in your head have never really been that useful; you just thought they were.

Your deeper self is real. It's alive. It *is* what is experiencing life through you. It's the realest thing that is here. It is more real than anything else. But you have to spend some time experiencing it before it becomes real to you, before it is realized by you. This is a process. It takes time.

Surrendering your thoughts is not as hard as it might seem. First you have to become aware of your thoughts. Many people are not even aware of what they're thinking. They are lost in their thoughts, but they are not actually aware of what they are thinking. Being lost in thought is not awareness. Awareness is the capacity to be objective about the thoughts you are thinking, to observe them, to be able to step aside from thought and see: "Oh, I'm thinking those thoughts."

Who is this "I" that is thinking these thoughts, and who is the "I" that can see the thoughts? This "I" that can see the thoughts is the real you. It is the intelligence that you are. It is able to observe the human experience. It's able to observe thoughts rather than be lost in them. This capacity to observe thought develops over the course of your spiritual evolution, and it's sped up by having a practice of meditation.

So the first step in being able to surrender your thoughts is being able to observe them. Then you have some choice about what you do with them. Will you believe them? Are they true? Are they helpful? All of those questions can be asked once you are aware of your thoughts. So that is the next step to surrendering thought and becoming free of it. First you are aware of your thoughts, and then you can inquire: Are they true? Are they useful? Do I need this thought?

Then when you see that most of your thoughts are not very true and not very useful, you are empowered to make another choice: to give your attention to something other than the mental realm — to reality, to the here and now experience you are having. To the mind, this seems very boring: "Why would I want to do that? Nothing's happening. I'm just washing the es. I'm just walking the dog. I'm just chopping this apple. What's the big deal? It's not very interesting." That's the mind's perspective.

But there is another perspective, and when you drop out of the mind, you can begin to experience this other perspective. You can experience the richness that your being experiences as it's chopping the apple or walking the dog or doing any of the other mundane things you do every day.

Your being loves to be alive. It loves to chop apples. It loves to clean the house. It loves to do everything. When you drop out of the mind that doesn't love to do those things and into your deeper self, you discover a great love for life, a great enjoyment of very simple things, little things. Every little thing is wonderful. You're satisfied with much less. Your desires are much less.

But that doesn't mean you won't have an abundant life, because when you are aligned with your deeper self, you are also aligned with love and goodness. And love and goodness bring you great abundance. When you express love and goodness, you will naturally receive that back, and much more. This place of love, simplicity, and contentment also has the potential for you to create and have a very beautiful, wonderful, comfortable, prosperous, and safe life. Everything the ego has wanted and tried to get through thought is available—much more available— when you are present to your deepest self, because your deepest self knows how to get these things, and it naturally attracts these things.

So when you surrender your thoughts, what you get is so much more. This surrender is a key to happiness, and it is necessary before you are able to fall in love with life. Because the egoic mind is the creator and generator of unhappiness, dissatisfaction, and discontentment, until you surrender this voice in your head, that is what you'll have: discontentment, dissatisfaction, unhappiness, fear, and desires for things that you don't have (which is painful). This is the egoic experience. It's not pretty. It's difficult. It's a place of suffering.

This place of suffering is created by thoughts in your head. If you are willing to surrender those thoughts, you will find a different life, and that life will be everything your ego ever wanted and so much more. Life is good, and you are meant to discover this. It's full, it's complete, and it supports you beautifully. This is what you are here to discover. You're here to find out what it is that blocks peace, love, and happiness. You're here to discover the cause of suffering, and in seeing that, you become free of suffering.

There is a way out of suffering. What you have to give up to no longer suffer is nothing tangible at all — just thoughts, just ideas about who "I" am and what "I" want and what "I" need and who "I" was in the past and who "I" will be in the future. Are you willing to give up these thoughts about "I"? You will still be here, you will still be living your life, you will still take action, and you will still speak. Nothing really changes, but everything changes.

When you change the place you live from, everything changes. When you begin to live from the present moment, from the deepest self, everything changes. And yet, you may still be in your life in the usual way, and perhaps other people will barely notice. They'll just think: "Oh, that person is really nice. That person is happy. What's her secret?"

You are here to be happy. You are here to live a full, happy, and complete life. You are here to find this happiness, this peace, and this joy, and you're here to express it in the world. Your life will completely change when you discover that you are not the "I" that you think you are and you realize the self that you really are.

CHAPTER 5
Silence

Silence is a means for becoming aligned with Presence. However, your environment doesn't need to be silent for you to align with Presence and experience it. Physical sound is not the problem; it is the inner talk from the voice in your head that needs to be silenced to come into alignment with Presence. For this to happen, it is often helpful to be quiet and not speak very much, which is why in many retreats silence is required. Speech tends to be the expression of the ego and the voice in your head. So if you suppress ordinary speech, you will stop reinforcing the egoic mind.

Any quieting of the body is also helpful for aligning with Presence, but not necessary of course. However, when the body is still, it becomes much easier to tune in to Presence and, more importantly, for the mind to settle and be quiet. When the body is settled and quiet, the mind becomes settled and quiet.

So there is a correlation between a quiet body-mind and mouth and the capacity to align with Presence.

Silence is actually another word for Presence. This is because when you are quiet in your body and mind, what remains is your true nature, and your true nature is experienced as silence, although this Silence isn't actually completely silent. There is a subtle pitch or hum to it that people can tune in to when everything else is quiet.

The Silence of your being is rich. It is actually full and complete, not empty or uninteresting, as the mind would have you think. To the mind, Silence is boring, uninteresting, and empty, and there's nothing going on. But when you are fully quiet and present to the Silence within, that Silence feels very rich, very complete, and peaceful. You feel content. Nothing is missing, nothing is needed. Isn't that what you all would like to feel—that there is nothing you need and nothing you have to have to be happy and content?

This experience of contentment is actually available to you always in any moment, but you have to turn away from the egoic mind, the voice in your head, which is not content, and just notice the silent contentment of your being. To do that, as I said, it is helpful to bring the body and mind into a more quiet place by just sitting and doing nothing, by not stimulating the mind, and by bringing your attention into the body and away from thought.

If a thought comes up, just notice it, and then bring your attention back to just being in the body here and now, to just this. What is the body experiencing? When you are very still and quiet, your body-mind will experience Silence, and the longer you stay in the Silence, the deeper it becomes, the more rich and rewarding it becomes.

It is possible for you to eventually move into quite a thoughtless place. This thoughtless place is extremely rewarding. It is where you go each night when you drop into deep sleep. How refreshing that is—to lose yourself in deep sleep, to know nothing, to think nothing, to be nothing. This is what is called *samadhi*.

Samadhi is absorption in the Silence to the point where there is no thought and no sense of self, just simple being. This is the goal of meditation, to arrive at a place of no thought or where thought is in the distance and impersonal. How ironic it is that the goal—the freedom—is to actually lose yourself, to lose your thoughts about yourself and the stream of thought that accompanies your every move.

What a relief it is to be quiet, to experience quiet, and to know yourself as this Silence. This is the goal of spiritual practice. You could say that it is the goal of life: to return Home again to this place of simplicity and quiet beingness without concern for "me," "myself," and "I" and to know yourself as everything and nothing at the same time. You are here to discover that you *are* this Silence, that you are this nothingness and this everything-ness, this boundary-less space that includes everything and loves everything. This is the great good news you are meant to discover.

You discover this largely through a practice of meditation. There are very few things in life that will bring you to this place more rapidly than meditation. And yet, the process of returning Home is hardly rapid. It can be a very slow process. It is slow for most people, but it is where you are all going.

The more time you spend in Silence, the more this experience is supported and reinforced, the more you will want to be there, and the more it will become familiar and the place from which you live. Then you will be able to bring Silence into your daily life more and more readily. You can begin to embody this Silence. As you go about your day, you can keep in touch with it. So with a practice of meditation, you develop a capacity to touch into Silence and become familiar with it and make it your own. Silence becomes part of your day and part of your way of being in the world. It will change how you are in the world like nothing else.

You can read books, you can study, you can learn things, but nothing will replace meditation. Meditation trains you to step into the Silence and stay in the Silence. Ultimately, it is the way for you to *be* Silence as you go about your day, to be the true self. If you can stay in touch with Silence during your day, your choices will come from Silence. Your actions and your words will come from Silence.

The point of knowing Silence is so that it can permeate your life, so that you can bring it into this world, which so badly needs it, and so that you are attuned to Silence in a way that allows it to determine your actions and speech. When you stay in touch with Silence, you will surely fulfill your life purpose in the most easeful and most fulfilling way. Everyone fulfills their life purpose to some extent, but the more you are aligned with Silence, the better you are able to fulfill your purpose.

The peace and contentment you receive from Silence is not meant for just you. It is meant for everyone. It is meant for you to share in this world with everyone, to spread the Silence of your being, which is transmitted to others. This is how consciousness is raised and evolution sped up. Those who know Silence transmit Silence so that others can learn Silence. That's another way you become accustom to Silence, besides meditation: Silence is received by you from someone who is a transmitter, from a teacher who lives in Silence.

If one spends enough time in Silence, he or she can't help but become a transmitter of Silence. So you can get a taste of Silence from someone else. Like a tuning fork, they tune you to their vibration when you are in touch with them. This is the role of a spiritual master or guru. There are many people on the planet today who are capable of transmitting this way. So these are two ways to become familiar with Silence: You experience it with a spiritual master or guru, or you meditate and find the Silence within. Both of these are time-honored ways of raising your consciousness, of evolving, of aligning with Presence.

Listening to the Silence as you meditate is a way of staying in Silence. As long as you are listening to the silent hum of your being, you won't be listening to your mind. Or if you are listening to the sounds in your environment, which is another form of meditation, you won't be listening to the voice in your head. You can't listen fully to two things at once. If you are lost in the thought-stream, you'll miss out on the Silence. But if you are listening to the Silence intently, the thought-stream will fall into the background.

The thought-stream doesn't have to completely disappear for you to stay with the Silence. It only has to drop into the background so that you're not involved with it. Or if you become involved with it, just bring your attention back to the Silence within or to the sounds in the environment, which can serve the same purpose.

The sounds in the environment are like a bridge to Silence. Focusing on sound focuses your mind and brings it out of involvement with the voice in your head and into involvement with the physical sound. If you stay with that physical sound long enough, you will lose yourself in that sound. You will lose the small self, the false self, the whole sense of "me," "myself," and "I."

Focusing on sound this way is a wonderful meditation. It will naturally drop you into the Silence. So if you are having difficulty tuning in to the Silence, then first tune in to the sounds in your environment. Become very curious about every sound. Notice it and then listen for the next sound. Listen to the spaces in between the sounds in your environment. Get curious—what will be next? Listen as if your life depended on it—your spiritual life does.

When you listen this intently—when you give all of your focus to the sound— at a certain point, you will find yourself aligned with Silence. In the space in between the sounds that you're listening to, you'll notice the Silence. That experience of Silence will grow and deepen.

So dear ones, know that Silence is always at hand. Even if there is noise in your environment, there is Silence in between the noise, underneath the noise, along with the noise. The sounds in your environment are not a problem. It's the sounds in your own head that are a problem. They are the only thing that can keep you from the Silence, because the voice in your head creates a sense of "I," a false sense of "I" that fascinates you, that tells stories, that suffers. That false self doesn't exist in the Silence. When you move out of these thoughts about yourself, you are left with the true spaciousness of your being.

So instead of being fascinated with the thoughts that are running through your mind, become fascinated by the Silence. Listen intently, carefully, and curiously to this Silence and see what you can discover. What you discover is actually an experience. As you listen intently to Silence, you go more deeply into Silence. The discovery is the discovery of the depths of Silence. You discover that there is no end to the depth of this Silence. It becomes absorbing.

The Silence absorbs your attention. It fascinates you in a way that is different from the fascination of the mind. You become transfixed on the Silence. This absorption in the Silence until you lose all interest in the voice in your head is a very good sign. Then you experience what it's like to just be, without any sense of "me," "myself," or "I," just pure, spacious beingness.

Every one of you is able to experience this. Every one of you *will* experience this. It is your destiny to experience your true nature. Those of you on this spiritual path are seeking for a purpose. Know that you can be a finder. Know that it is for you to find, to discover who you are. Know it and, more importantly, express it, be it in the world. This is a wonderful journey. It is a process that unfolds over time. It takes time to get to know yourself. It takes time to learn to embody and express it in the world.

You are being guided every step of the way by those on other dimensions who deeply love you. Know that they rejoice in every step you take on this path. Every moment you spend meditating and every effort you take to know yourself as Silence, experience Silence, and be Silence is worthwhile and supported. Know that you are deeply loved, and we are all rooting for you and for your happiness, peace, and contentment.

You are never alone. In the Silence, you know all of this. It's when you are not in the Silence that you need to be reminded and encouraged, because it is so very difficult when you are caught up in the egoic mind to remember the truth, to be the truth. It can be so very difficult to be a human being. So please know that we understand and have compassion for the difficulties you experience. We know it is no easy task to awaken out of the egoic mind. But you are beautiful and strong beings, and you are doing it. Simply by reading or listening to this, you are taking a step. You are affirming your desire to awaken. So please continue, knowing that you are receiving all the support you need in every moment.

CHAPTER 6
A Guided Meditation
on Silence

Note: Here is a guided meditation that you can record for yourself and listen to. The audiobook, of course, includes a recording of it. You can find out about the audiobook here:

www.RadicalHappiness.com/audio-video/jesus-channelings

Settle into a comfortable place. Reclining is just fine. Be as comfortable as you can be so that you can give your full attention to these words. First, take a moment to notice how your body feels in whatever position you're in. There's a place where your body meets whatever you are sitting or reclining on. Just notice these areas where your body is touching whatever is holding your body up. Notice how your body is held and supported by whatever it is held and supported by. Just notice that now for a moment. Give your full attention to the experience of the body being supported.

Keep noticing this as I continue speaking to you. This support that you're feeling is present in every moment of your life, not only physically, but in other ways. This physical support is a metaphor, you could say, for how you are always receiving the support you need from the universe, which deeply loves and cherishes you. Why would it not support that which it loves? You only have to notice this support for a moment to experience the gratitude that your being naturally has for this support and for simply existing. Your being is relishing existing and relishing in existence, every aspect of it.

Continue to sink more deeply into wherever you are resting. Notice the body relaxing even more fully into wherever you are. Right now, nothing else exists but this experience that your body is having and these words. Continue to give your full attention to *just this.*

It is simple to give your attention to this experience. When you do, you discover that giving your attention to just this is actually very interesting. You don't know what I'm going to say next, and you can notice a natural curiosity about that. Your being is curious about what will happen next. What will be said next? How will it feel? What will that experience be like? Your being notices the littlest things and finds them enthralling, lovely, perfect. There is total peace and contentment in this simple curiosity and appreciation of how life is unfolding simply and perfectly in this moment. This moment has its own timing, unfoldment, and flavor, and it couldn't be otherwise. It can only be as it is.

The unfolding of the moment is often covered over by thoughts about it. If thoughts arise, just set them aside for a while and continue to notice what is unfolding now, in *this* moment: What sounds are arising? Just listen for a few minutes and see what you can hear. Be sure to also notice the silence in between the sounds.

Besides sounds, what sensations are here? What other sensations are there besides those of your body resting and breathing? Can you feel, or sense, more subtle energetic sensations, aliveness, energy flowing, tingles, prickles, or other very subtle sensations? You have to pay very close attention to catch these.

Your being is fascinated by the ever-changing panoply of life. Everything is being carried out as needed by your body and by your surroundings. Life is taking care of life just perfectly. Take a few minutes to just be with and fully experience any sensations you are experiencing.

Now I want you to begin to notice something even more subtle than all these sounds and sensations. I want you to notice the space, the Silence, in between the sounds and sensations, the space in which the sounds and sensations are happening. The space is actually very full and not empty at all. The space is actually *something*, not nothing. So notice it and just see what you can discover about it. Give it your full attention, as if nothing else in the world existed or mattered. Become very curious about it. Take several minutes now and just notice this space, this Silence, in which everything else is arising.

Can you find a place where you stop and the space begins? Your body exists in this space and seems to stop at the surface of your skin, but you are not your body, are you? Aren't you, rather, the consciousness that is aware of your body and everything else? Is that consciousness separate from the space? Can you find a place where your consciousness stops and that space begins? Aren't your consciousness and the space the same thing? Aren't you awash in an ocean of consciousness, or space, in which there are no boundaries between you and this space?

You are the silent awareness that we call Silence, with a capital S. You are what is silently aware of everything, silently existing and silently experiencing life. This silent Watcher or Witness doesn't comment on life. It doesn't put forth opinions. It doesn't separate life into concepts, like black and white, good and bad. In this Silence, there are no concepts, no thoughts, only purity of being and complete acceptance of life just as it is.

This acceptance is an embrace of all that is, without qualifications or conditions. This space, this Silence, allows everything to happen in it and everything to be experienced. Its nature is to allow, to love, to embrace everything. And that is your nature. Deep within you, beyond all thoughts and concepts is the "you" that is Silent, allowing, accepting, loving, and all-embracing. In any moment, it is possible for you to align with Silence and experience it rejoicing in life, in every little experience, even every difficult experience.

You are not your thoughts. Your thoughts do not belong to you, but to your human self. They are the programming that makes you human, that makes you believe you are your thoughts and only your thoughts, the programming that prevents you from seeing what you truly are.

This life is a game of hide and seek. Your true nature is hidden from you, and you are meant to discover it. You discover it by silencing your mind, your thoughts, and looking to see what else is here. What is here that is more subtle than thought? What is here that is aware of all thoughts and of everything else? You are this silent space, this silent watcher who loves life

CHAPTER 7
Giving

One's willingness to give is a testament to their willingness to trust life. Giving is not natural to the ego. Giving is something that comes from a deeper state, from the true self, which is connected to All That Is. When you know that you are connected to and part of All That Is, it's natural to give. Giving and love naturally flow from the realization of who you really are and of what life really is. When you realize that you *are* life and that life is giving to itself through you, then giving comes naturally.

But it is not natural to humans to give in this way. What is natural to humans is what they are programmed to do, which is to take care of themselves, to look out for #1. It's natural to believe that scarcity prevails in this world and that if you give you might not have, when quite the opposite is true: When you give, you will have, because there is a natural law that giving must evoke the same. And the opposite is true:

Withholding evokes withholding from life. This is one of the ways you learn about the truth about life. Life shows you what is true by delivering to you what you put out.

When you give, when you are generous of spirit, and when you love, that's what you experience inside yourself, and that also comes back to you from outside yourself. A loving person is someone who is loved; an unloving person is someone who is unloved. You create your reality in this way. You create your inner experience of reality. By being unloving, you experience a lack of love, and that draws to you the same: an ungenerosity of spirit from the world.

When you are not generous and not loving, you are vibrating at a certain level, and then those who have a similar vibration are attracted to you. If you are vibrating negativity, then you will attract those who are vibrating negativity. If you are vibrating at a higher level, such as love, generosity, peace, or compassion, then you will attract those who are vibrating at that same level.

Each of you lives in a world populated by people of a similar vibration, because you will naturally move in circles of people who are similar to you. If you are vibrating at a higher level, those like you will be attracted to you, and you will not gravitate toward those who are vibrating at a lower level, except perhaps to be of service to them, to help them.

When you are vibrating at a higher level, you don't say yes to everyone who comes to you. You give to those you feel moved to give to from a deeper place, and move away from those who would tend to bring you into a lower vibration and not benefit from association with you. So vibrating at a higher vibration does not mean you will mingle with or serve everyone who comes your way. You will know who you are meant to serve and who you are not meant to serve. It will be clear, because from a place of alignment with your true self, it is clear who you are to serve and not serve. So you move accordingly.

Those who are vibrating at a lower level have lessons with others who are vibrating at a lower level. This is one of the ways you learn to change your thoughts and behavior and beliefs — through association with others who hold your negative beliefs and share your negative perceptions and feelings. You suffer together, and at some point, you see that you can wake up out of this suffering. You look around and see who is not suffering and wonder why it is they're not suffering and you are.

There are hells on this earth, in a sense, created by negativity, by negative perceptions and incorrect beliefs. Through living in this hellish environment, eventually people learn to wake up from it. They receive feedback about their own negative beliefs and learn about them through others who share them. This is how growth is accomplished.

Negativity can be turned around by beginning to trust that goodness, giving, and love are the way to peace and happiness. Not everyone is convinced of that. People are following their fears and their desires for power and material wealth, for things. In following your ego's desires and fears, you get only that: more fear, more desire. There is no end to fear and desire. Your fear is never assuaged, and your desires are never satisfied. There are always more fears and more desires. When you follow the path of the ego, you are never done: You are never good enough, you never have enough, others are never good enough, and others never give you enough.

There has to be another way to see life. And so there is. Fortunately, there is another way, which does bring peace, happiness, and love. The way to get peace, happiness, and love is not to look for them outside of yourself, to go after them in the form of power or money. The way to get happiness, peace, and love is to *be* peace, happiness, and love, to find them and experience them within yourself and then to express them in the world.

How do you find peace, happiness, and love within yourself when you are not experiencing them? The only reason you would not be experiencing them is because your mind is keeping you from experiencing them by telling you lies about yourself and about life. If you stop listening to the lies that your egoic mind is telling you, you will find the truth. You will find the peace, love, and happiness within you. It is only the thoughts in your head that keep you from experiencing these things.

You are innately loving. Your innate nature is covered over — that's all. The goodness within you is who you are. You are goodness. Your mind tells you otherwise. It tells you what you are: "I'm this, I'm that, I like this and I don't like that, I feel this way and I don't feel that way." Your mind creates a pretend self with all of these "I" thoughts. If you believe these "I" thoughts, you become that limited, small, imagination of a self. And when you believe yourself to be that self, you act accordingly, and other people believe you to be that self as well.

This is how the false self is created, simply by all of the ideas you have about yourself: "I can't do this. I'm not like that. I'm weak. I'm unworthy. I'm not good enough. I can't compete. I always fail." These thoughts create that reality. They create, first, the inner experience of unworthiness and also the experience of unhappiness and all the other feelings that follow from the belief "I'm not worthy." The sadness, the shame—all of the negative feelings—come from the limited thoughts about "I."

You can't say a single thing about this "I" that would contain the whole truth about who you are. Anything you say about "I," except "I exist," is a lie to one extent or another because it doesn't adequately describe who you are. Who you really are is very mysterious and capable of all sorts of things you've never dreamed of.

The "I" is made up of imaginary beliefs you have about yourself, things others have told you about yourself or you've imagine or concluded about yourself when you were a small and powerless child. Children naturally conclude negative things about themselves because they are not very capable as children. How could they be? They're not strong—how could they be? They're not so smart—how could they be? They don't know the ways of life yet. Children fail all the time. Children do things poorly all the time.

So, dear ones, you get stuck in the past in your beliefs about yourself. You think you are still the child who can't, the child who isn't able to keep up with the adults. You carry around this image of yourself as the powerless and incapable child that you once were. It's natural, of course. This happens to all children. It can't be any other way, given the way your brain works and given the way culture works. These ideas become imprinted, and you believe them.

So you need to look at the ideas you have about yourself. You need to examine the old ideas and see how true they are—how false they are and how inadequate they are to describe you. This is how you see through the false self. You look at the ideas you have about yourself and ask: "Is that true? Do I need that? Is that useful? Is that serving me? Is that serving life?"

It doesn't serve life for you to be limited. It serves life for you to be in touch with your fullest potential, with the love and kindness at your core, the joy at your core. This is what serves life. It serves your life, and it serves everyone else's lives. Everyone else in the Whole benefits when you are aligned with your true self and not your false self.

The people around you might be upset if you don't agree with their perceptions of you: "You should be this way. You should be like I think you are. You should be like my imagination of you." But you can't live your life as an expression of someone else's imagination. That isn't fair to you, it isn't fair to life, and it isn't even fair to them. So you have to move beyond these false conceptions of yourself and be strong and courageous enough to know that you are greater than any idea you could hold about yourself.

You exist as existence, as life, as love, as beingness, which is the same beingness that is behind all of life and behind every being. When you align with this, you will be happy; and when you are happy, love flows; and when love flows, others are happy and feel good; and when they feel good, love flows from them. And so this is how the world is changed. You must change it within yourself first. You must become the loving being that you actually are. Know it, be it, and express it, and everything else in your life will fall into place.

You don't have to figure out how you will survive or what you will do. All of that will come about and unfold naturally, because this being that you are, which is behind all of life, is supremely wise and intelligent. It wants you to survive, to flourish, to be happy, to be loving, and to be at peace. And when you agree to that, it will give you everything you really want and everything you really need. I say "really" because you won't necessarily receive everything your ego wants or thinks it needs to be happy, but you will be given a beautiful life, the life you are meant to live, the life you are meant to grow and evolve from.

Each of you is here for a certain reason. That life will be unfolded the more you are aligned with peace, happiness, and love. Having and living that life *is* happiness. When you are living the life you are meant to live—whatever that might be and however that might look—you will be happy and content. Your soul came here to fulfill a certain purpose, and when you are fulfilling that, you are deeply happy and deeply fulfilled, and that is enough. You won't need other things on top of that to feel alright. So much of what the ego wants is a pacifier for all the pain it feels. You won't need those pacifiers, those addictions, those pleasures to get by in life. You'll be too busy doing what you love to do.

Giving is how you turn it all around from the ego's world to living in a place of contentment, peace, and joy. Giving is the key to turning it around. Giving is a way of acknowledging that you trust the goodness within you. You trust it enough to express it, and you trust it to take care of you. You trust that giving is the way to live. Giving acknowledges that you believe that love is behind life, that love is the key to life. You are willing to give because you believe this. This is an appropriate belief.

So many of your ego's beliefs take you in the opposite direction. But believe that giving—love—is the answer, and you will discover that it is. You will discover the deepest truth about life: that life is good and that it is unfolded most beautifully by aligning with the goodness and love within you and expressing that in the world.

Giving is how you align with the unfolding of your life, which is already happening. It is how you draw abundance and everything you need to you. The ego's way is the opposite, and it doesn't work very well. Just look around you, and you can see that the world doesn't work very well. Going about life in a selfish, me-first way does not make the wheels of this world turn well. This causes a lot of strife, conflict, and unhappiness.

It doesn't have to be this way. You don't have to be out for yourself. The best way to take care of yourself is to be generous, kind, compassionate, and considerate, even when others are not. You can't afford to be otherwise, really. It only causes more strife and unhappiness. This world can't afford the luxury of more pain. It can't afford to go in the direction of the ego.

The way this is turned around is by turning this around within yourself, by committing to love and believing that love is the answer, that being generous of spirit is the answer to your life and to this world's problems.

So please turn this around within yourselves. Turn this around. You are the only one who can do this. It is a choice you make about your beliefs. Do you believe your "I" thoughts? Do you believe what the ego says to you? Or do you believe that love and goodness are the answer?

You choose. Your choice determines your experience and the experience in the world. It is a choice, what to believe. When you are as conscious as you are—and certainly you are or you wouldn't be reading or listening to this—you are conscious enough to choose. Not everyone is, but you are conscious enough to choose. So you must do that. It falls on you to do that.

How to Give

How and when to give are the biggest questions. Your mind doesn't know when to give. Your egoic mind has rules and other beliefs and ideas about when to give and how much and whether to give. The egoic mind is run by the ego, and the ego is not giving. So when the ego can get away with not giving, it will not give. But if it has conditioning that says, "You should give," then you will feel compelled to follow that conditioning if you are listening to your mind.

There is something deeper to listen to that knows how and when to give. The key to learning to give wisely is to first give your attention to the present moment, to what is arising here and now on deep and subtle levels of your being. Specifically, is there joy in the idea of giving something in this moment? Does giving naturally flow out of the moment, and does it flow joyfully from you, as a yes? Or is it a no? Is your being giving you a sense of "No, it's not time to give"?

Your being will tell you how to give and when to give, but you have to listen on more subtle levels to the signs and signals your being gives, which aren't words, like the egoic mind. Rather, a subtle sense of yes or no will tell you whether it's time to give something and how much.

Always the key is to follow your joy, follow the yes inside. There can also be a no inside, but it's not a verbal yes or a verbal no, or a should or a should not. This yes or no comes out of the flow in the moment. When a request or need arises in your environment, you either say yes to it or no spontaneously, automatically, naturally. Your being responds naturally to life. It responds without thinking.

Sometimes the mind intervenes and changes that response or blocks it, but always your being is communicating with you about what is a yes and what is a no, what direction to go in, how to move, and what to say. Your being continually communicates this to you in subtle ways through joy, a sense of yes, an openness, and a willingness or a sense of closed-ness and withdrawal. You can learn to read and listen to these signs and respond to them.

Life comes out of the moment. Your responses to life come out of the moment naturally, spontaneously, and without thought. Something happens, and your being responds. It says yes to it or no to it. That's it. It's that simple. It only gets complicated when the mind gets involved and questions that response: "Should I do that or not? If I do that, what will happen?" It strategizes and considers the results.

Your being just says yes or no without strategizing or thinking ahead. Your being knows how to live this life. It doesn't need to strategize. The plan is already in place, and your being is responding naturally to the life plan. In a sense, your being already has its orders; it already knows what direction to go in. It already knows what is a yes and what is a no. It doesn't have to think about it, consider it, weigh the pros and cons, strategize, or imagine the future, like the mind does.

You don't need to do these things. Your mind *thinks* you need to do these things, and there are times when it is useful to use your mind in that way. But for much of life, you can live from this place of moment-to-moment spontaneity. You align yourself with life by being in the moment, and you get into the moment by giving your attention to what is real and true now and to where your joy lies now.

The flow is always going in a direction of joy. You can follow your joy; you can follow this flow. That's the route you're meant to take. It will bring you happiness. It will bring you safety and security too. This joy is not only joyful; it's safe. It is what is leading you to unfold the life you are meant to live.

The only thing that can interfere with living the life you are meant to live is living the life the egoic mind thinks you should be living, which is essentially a conditioned life, a life lived according to what others think you should do. Do others know what you should do? How could they? They aren't you. Only you know what you "should" do, and you know this by following your joy and also by following a sense of contraction or no when that occurs on a subtle, deep level.

So this is how life is lived. It's lived very simply from the present moment by giving your attention to the present moment. That is the first kind of giving you need to do: Give your attention to the present moment, to what is real and true and arising right now in the present moment. That will tell you what you need to do to fulfill your life plan, to be loving, to be peaceful, and to live a happy life.

Give your attention to the present moment. Do not give it to the voice in your head. Turn your attention away from the voice in your head to what is arising here and now in this moment. Get into your body and senses so that you can experience the more subtle realm of the present moment. This is the realm in which your being lives and expresses itself, the realm in which it communicates its direction to you.

All of you know what it's like to live in alignment with yourself because there are many times in your day when you already do that. This being that you are *is* what is living your life, and many moments out of the day, it is moving simply and spontaneously through life without thought. Many of your actions are already done spontaneously without thought.

There is an innate wisdom that is living you, which is the life force, the true self. It's here, now, living you. When you believe you are the false self, however, that takes over, the ideas in your head take over, and you live out that life, the life of the false self.

So in some moments, you are living the life of the false self, and that's fine. It brings you experiences and lessons, which your being is happy to have. Your being is willing to have any experience you choose from the level of your ego. It doesn't mind having experiences. But some of the experiences your ego chooses lead to suffering. Of course, your being doesn't mind that either.

However, you can live life much more gracefully if you simply drop out of your egoic mind and into this flow of your being and let *it* live you, let it move you, let it speak you, allow it to be what propels you through life — because it is already doing that, and it will do it in more moments if only you allow it to.

When you do allow it to propel you in life, you find that it is a very giving force. It says yes and gives of itself in beautiful ways, in ways your mind would have never thought of doing. Your true self is loving, generous, and interested in serving others. If you let it, it will do this in many more moments during your day than you generally do. And it will know when to say no and when not to follow certain obligations or shoulds that your mind would press upon you. Some of those obligations and shoulds only drain you and don't really serve. Your inner wisdom is wise enough to know when something will serve and when it won't.

So to become the giving and loving being you are meant to be, first give your attention to the present moment. Drop into your body and senses and out of your mind. That will allow you to experience the subtle movement of your inner being, the direction that it is moving in and the joy that it is following. The yeses, the nos — they are all there on a subtle level for you to follow.

When I say that giving is important and the key to happiness, I don't mean that you should be giving in every moment. That would be too draining. To give appropriately, you need to give your attention to the here and now so that you can attune to what your being is naturally saying yes and no to. This is the truest giving, the most appropriate giving, and it will bring you and everyone around you the greatest happiness.

CHAPTER 8
Conclusion

You know the state of Grace — of Silence, of Presence — from when you were a very small child, before you had concepts for things and beliefs about things. You experienced this purity of being then, and you can experience it now. You needed to develop language, concepts, and a sense of identity. That was natural, part of your growth. The next stage of growth beyond that is going beyond concepts and beliefs to the experience of the purity of your being, but with a developed sense of self and an ability to reason and communicate.

If you stay in this place of purity long enough, you will fall in love with life. You will fall in love with God, and you will know God as goodness. You will know yourself as this goodness, and you will know that this is all there is and all there ever has been. Any negativity or evil has been a forgetting of this goodness, a natural outcome of losing yourself in mistaken beliefs and misunderstandings.

This can be righted by correcting those misunderstandings, which I have in part attempted to do — to tell you the truth about life, that it is good, benevolent, bountiful, and supportive. When you know this in your heart of hearts, your experience of life and life, itself, for you will change. You can be happy, you can be free of fear and negativity, and that is where you are all headed.

Free yourself from your mistaken beliefs and misunderstandings, and you will be happy. This is such a simple teaching, and yet, it is so very difficult at times to do. Many of your beliefs are not in your awareness, and those that are, are often difficult to disbelieve. But that is the work: to question your assumptions about life and about yourself, question your negative thoughts, and begin to believe another set of beliefs, ones that are more in alignment with reality, with Truth.

To discover these beliefs, you must first come to know Reality, Truth. You must experience the truth about reality, not just intellectually agree with what I'm saying about it. The understanding is first accepted by your mind, and then it must be experienced. Then you will believe it, and then you will be able to begin to live it, to express it in this world. You experience it by being very present in the moment.

To know Reality, you have to be brave enough to step beyond your conceptions about life — what you have been told about life by your religions — and discover for yourself what is true. Don't take other people's beliefs as true without first examining them to see if they stand up to Truth: Do they make you happier, more loving, more at peace? This is the test. Beliefs that don't help you live as I taught two thousand years ago cannot serve you today. Humanity is still struggling to live as I taught then, but today it is more possible than ever to live in peace, love, and prosperity with your fellow human beings.

This may seem wildly impossible given the state of the world, but given the state of the world, it becomes necessary — indeed imperative — that you find a way to live in peace with each other. Time is running out for humanity. It is at a crossroads: Will you destroy yourselves with nuclear weapons or come together as one family of humankind?

How many more wars will it take before the futility of war is seen and the wisdom of sharing your wealth with others is adopted as the obvious solution? Shower others with food supplies, gifts, medical help, and other necessary commodities instead of bombs. This is your only hope. Giving is the answer, not conflict or grasping to your national interests. It is hatred fomented by differing religious beliefs and other differences that is the basis of war.

Question your beliefs, and don't let any belief interfere with seeing others as yourself and giving to others as yourself. How can a belief that does not lead to love and unity rightfully belong to any religion or ideology? That is a flawed religion or ideology.

Don't try to change other people's beliefs; you will never succeed. Live according to love, and people will change in their regard of you. Do not try to conquer others but win them over with love, generosity, compassion, and understanding. If these are the keys to your own personal happiness—and they are—they are also the keys to humanity's happiness. This was my message two thousand years ago, and it is my message today. It was revolutionary then, and it is revolutionary now. I speak to you today with this very same message: Love one another! Change yourself, and then change the world.

Information about and links to purchase the audiobook of this book, *Jesus Speaking: On Falling in Love with Life*, are here:

www.RadicalHappiness.com/audio-video/jesus-channelings

If you enjoyed this book, we think you will enjoy
these other books by Gina Lake:

*All Grace: New Teachings from Jesus on the Truth
About Life.* Grace is the mysterious and unseen
movement of God upon creation, which is motivated
by love and indistinct from love. *All Grace* was given to
Gina Lake by Jesus and represents his wisdom and
understanding of life. It is about the magnificent and
incomprehensible force behind life, which created life,
sustains it, and operates within it as you and me and
all of creation. *All Grace* is full of profound and life-
changing truth.

*In the World but Not of It: New Teachings from Jesus
on Embodying the Divine:* From the Introduction by
Jesus: "What I have come to teach now is that you can
embody love, as I did. You can become Christ within
this human life and learn to embody all that is good
within you. I came to show you the beauty of your own
soul and what is possible as a human. I came to show
you that it is possible to be both human and divine, to
be love incarnate. You are equally both. You walk with
one foot in the world of form and another in the
Formless. This mysterious duality within your being is
what this book is about." This book is another in a
series of books dictated to Gina Lake by Jesus.

ABOUT the AUTHOR

Gina Lake is a spiritual teacher and the author of over twenty books about awakening to one's true nature, including *All Grace, In the World but Not of It, The Jesus Trilogy, A Heroic Life, From Stress to Stillness, Trusting Life, Embracing the Now, Radical Happiness,* and *Choosing Love.* She is also a gifted intuitive with a master's degree in counseling psychology and over twenty-five years' experience supporting people in their spiritual growth. Her website offers information about her books and online courses, a free e-book, a blog, and audio and video recordings:

www.RadicalHappiness.com

The Radical Happiness Online Course

Meditation will change your life because meditation changes your brain like nothing else can. Find out how. Get serious about waking up and becoming happier. The Radical Happiness online course will show you how and get you started. This 8-week course, which can be begun anytime, will provide you with a foundation for awakening and increase your happiness through spiritual practices, a structure for doing those practices, and support from an online forum. This course uses a combination of written text, instructional audios, guided meditations, inquiries, and exercises. The practices include four types of meditation, spiritual inquiry, breathing practices, a gratitude practice, love and forgiveness practices, prayer, and others. For more information, please visit:

www.RadicalHappiness.com/courses

More Books by Gina Lake

Available in paperback, ebook, and audiobook
formats.

From Stress to Stillness: Tools for Inner Peace. Most
stress is created by how we think about things. *From
Stress to Stillness* will help you to examine what you are
thinking and change your relationship to your
thoughts so that they no longer result in stress.
Drawing from the wisdom traditions, psychology,
New Thought, and the author's own experience as a
spiritual teacher and counselor, *From Stress to Stillness*
offers many practices and suggestions that will lead to
greater peace and equanimity, even in a busy and
stress-filled world.

Radical Happiness: A Guide to Awakening provides
the keys to experiencing the happiness that is ever-
present and not dependent on circumstances. This
happiness doesn't come from getting what you want,
but from wanting what is here now. It comes from
realizing that who you think you are is not who you
really are. This is a radical perspective! *Radical
Happiness* describes the nature of the egoic state of
consciousness and how it interferes with happiness,
what awakening and enlightenment are, and how to
live in the world after awakening.

Embracing the Now: Finding Peace and Happiness in What Is. The Now—this moment—is the true source of happiness and peace and the key to living a fulfilled and meaningful life. *Embracing the Now* is a collection of essays that can serve as daily reminders of the deepest truths. Full of clear insight and wisdom, *Embracing the Now* explains how the mind keeps us from being in the moment, how to move into the Now and stay there, and what living from the Now is like. It also explains how to overcome stumbling blocks to being in the Now, such as fears, doubts, misunderstandings, judgments, distrust of life, desires, and other conditioned ideas that are behind human suffering.

Choosing Love: Moving from Ego to Essence in Relationships. Having a truly meaningful relationship requires choosing love over your conditioning, that is, your ideas, fantasies, desires, images, and beliefs. *Choosing Love* describes how to move beyond conditioning, judgment, anger, romantic illusions, and differences to the experience of love and Oneness with another. It explains how to drop into the core of your Being, where Oneness and love exist, and be with others from there.

Living in the Now: How to Live as the Spiritual Being That You Are. The 99 essays in *Living in the Now* will help you realize your true nature and live as that. They answer many questions raised by the spiritual search and offer wisdom on subjects such as fear, anger, happiness, aging, boredom, desire, patience, faith, forgiveness, acceptance, love, commitment, hope, purpose, meaning, meditation, being present, emotions, trusting life, trusting your Heart, and many other deep subjects. These essays will help you become more conscious, present, happy, loving, grateful, at peace, and fulfilled. Each essay stands on its own and can be used for daily contemplation.

Trusting Life: Overcoming the Fear and Beliefs That Block Peace and Happiness. Fear and distrust keep us from living the life we were meant to live, and they are the greatest hurdles to seeing the truth about life — that it is good, abundant, supportive, and potentially joyous. *Trusting Life* is a deep exploration into the mystery of who we are, why we suffer, why we don't trust life, and how to become more trusting. It offers evidence that life is trustworthy and tools for overcoming the fear and beliefs that keep us from falling in love with life.

The Jesus Trilogy. In this trilogy by Jesus, are three jewels, each shining in its own way and illuminating the same truth: You are not only human but divine, and you are meant to flourish and love one another. In words that are for today, Jesus speaks intimately and directly to the reader of the secrets to peace, love, and happiness. He explains the deepest of all mysteries: who you are and how you can live as he taught long ago. The three books in *The Jesus Trilogy* were dictated to Gina Lake by Jesus and include *Choice and Will, Love and Surrender, and Beliefs, Emotions,* and *the Creation of Reality.*

A Heroic Life: New Teachings from Jesus on the Human Journey. The hero's journey—this human life—is a search for the greatest treasure of all: the gifts of your true nature. These gifts are your birthright, but they have been hidden from you, kept from you by the dragon: the ego. These gifts are the wisdom, love, peace, courage, strength, and joy that reside at your core. *A Heroic Life* shows you how to overcome the ego's false beliefs and face the ego's fears. It provides you with both a perspective and a map to help you successfully and happily navigate life's challenges and live heroically. This book is another in a series of books dictated to Gina Lake by Jesus.

Return to Essence: How to Be in the Flow and Fulfill Your Life's Purpose describes how to get into the flow and stay there and how to live life from there. Being in the flow and not being in the flow are two very different states. One is dominated by the ego-driven mind, which is the cause of suffering, while the other is the domain of Essence, the Divine within each of us. You are meant to live in the flow. The flow is the experience of Essence—your true self—as it lives life through you and fulfills its purpose for this life.

Getting Free: Moving Beyond Negativity and Limiting Beliefs. To a large extent, healing our conditioning involves changing our relationship to our mind and discovering who we really are. *Getting Free* will help you do that. It will also help you reprogram your mind; clear negative thoughts and self-images; use meditation, prayer, forgiveness, and gratitude; work with spiritual forces to assist healing and clear negativity; and heal entrenched issues from the past.

For more info, please visit the "Books" page at
www.RadicalHappiness.com

Made in the USA
Middletown, DE
25 November 2017